AF323952

WHY MACHIAVELLI MATTERS

WHY MACHIAVELLI MATTERS

A Guide to Citizenship in a Democracy

John Bernard

Praeger Series on the Early Modern World
Raymond B. Waddington, Series Editor

PRAEGER

Westport, Connecticut
London

Library of Congress Cataloging-in-Publication Data

Bernard, John D.

Why Machiavelli matters : a guide to citizenship in a democracy / John Bernard.

p. cm. — (Praeger series on the early modern world, ISSN 1940–1523)

Includes bibliographical references and index.

ISBN 978-0-275-99876-9 (alk. paper)

1. Machiavelli, Niccolò, 1469–1527—Criticism and interpretation. 2. Machiavelli, Niccolò, 1469–1527—Political and social views. 3. Political science—Philosophy. I. Title.

JC143.M4B55   2009

320.01—dc22   2008032413

British Library Cataloguing in Publication Data is available.

Library of Congress Catalog Card Number: 2008032413
ISBN: 978-0-275-99876-9
ISSN: 1940-1523

First published in 2009

Praeger Publishers, 88 Post Road West, Westport, CT 06881
An imprint of Greenwood Publishing Group, Inc.
www.praeger.com

Printed in the United States of America

The paper used in this book complies with the Permanent Paper Standard issued by the National Information Standards Organization (Z39.48-1984).

10 9 8 7 6 5 4 3 2 1

For Artis, "friend
and dear friend"

Contents

PREFACE

This book has a dual purpose. On the one hand, it is a belated homage to a seminal thinker who has profoundly influenced my life. On the other hand, it is a plea by one concerned citizen to others to become actively engaged in preserving our precious democracy.

In my former vocation as an English professor, I spent over twenty-five years in a first-rate honors program (later college) at the University of Houston. Up to then, I had been a pretty straightforward specialist in Renaissance English poetry. But beginning in 1979, I spent a large part of my classroom time team-teaching a "Great Books" course to exceptionally bright freshmen and sophomores, in various areas of concentration, under the inspiring leadership of Ted Estess, director of the program, and later dean of the college.

Although I had read *The Prince* in college, my acquaintance with its author up to that time was shallow and my sense of him conventional. The program in which I then renewed the acquaintance was dominated by a succession of political theorists from schools like Chicago, Toronto, and Yale that were steeped in the tradition of Leo Strauss. The Straussian take on Machiavelli, relentlessly driven home to both students and neophyte professors, was not flattering. We took away two "facts" from the week or so devoted to Machiavelli: he was (in the master's phrase) a "teacher of evil," and—his one redeeming feature, I suppose—in the retiring years when he produced his wicked tome he communed with the wise men of antiquity. But the main thing we learned from this introduction to one of the world's great republican thinkers was the one thing everyone knew already: that Machiavelli was indeed "Machiavellian."

While repeating this academic ritual over two-and-a-half decades, I gradually developed my own reading of Machiavelli, aided by other colleagues with very different perspectives. Putting the text in its historical and biographical contexts, I came to read *The Prince* in more subtle ways. So when Machiavelli notes (in Chapter 5) that anyone who acquires a "city accustomed to freedom, and does not destroy it, may be expected to be destroyed by it"—a wicked one-liner guaranteed to arouse in Straussians a *frisson* of self-righteous indignation—it could be conceded that he is at least acknowledging the powerful hold that liberty has on those who enjoy it.

Even more telling were the circumstances in which the text came to be. Machiavelli had been a major player in the revived Florentine republic under his friend Piero Soderini. As second chancellor and secretary of the Ten while still only in his late twenties and early thirties, he combined the responsibilities of an American secretary of state and secretary of defense. Then, almost apocalyptically, on the Republic's dissolution and the restoration of the antirepublican Medici, Machiavelli found his occupation gone. Discharged from all his offices by the new regime, briefly imprisoned and tortured on the mistaken belief that he had joined a conspiracy against it, and finally consigned to a kind of house arrest on his farm twenty miles from Florence, he had no outlet for his patriotism—he would later famously write that "I love my country more than my own soul"—for the fifteen years' worth of practical political wisdom he had acquired in the Second Chancery, and perhaps most of all for the sharp wit and uncontainable energy his acquaintances consistently recorded.

Still, I had a career to pursue and books and articles on Renaissance literature to write. Only after retiring in Maine and reassessing my own life *post res perditas*—Machiavelli's phrase for the premature enforced retirement he faced at age thirty-four—did I begin to suspect that the old "prick," as his friends never tired of calling him, still had a hold on me. Having decided to reverse Machiavelli's pattern and dedicate my own declining years to civic engagement, I found my activism haunted by the spirit of his life and writings. When Maine's notorious "tax burden" was bemoaned in letters to the editor or in the halls of the state house, there Machiavelli would be, proclaiming that "well-ordered republics have to keep the public rich but their citizens poor." Or when the Thatcherian mantra sounded—anathema to my grassroots activist cohort—that "there is no community, there are only individuals," Machiavelli would be there to stubbornly counter, "it is not the well-being of individuals that makes cities great, but that of the community." Clearly, in the work I had chosen to do as a senior citizen, "Citizen Machiavelli" would be one of my spiritual mentors.

And so he has been, and a debt must be repaid. If Machiavelli matters to this citizen-activist in twenty-first-century America, then a public that mostly knows him about as well as I did when I started teaching him to honors students deserves to make his acquaintance and, if possible, be helped to acquire my own sense of what he has to tell us about life in a political community.

Here, of course, a problem arises. Despite the historical gap of nearly five hundred years—written in 1512–1513, *The Prince* was not published until 1532, five years after its author's death—Machiavelli's best-known work retains its wicked, if specious, glow. Even to those of us who have never read it, the familiar epithet "Machiavellian" derives from its sensational pages. But his other major works—the *Discourses*, the *Florentine Histories*, perhaps especially the public correspondence in his *Legations* and the private one in his *Letters*—are even less accessible. True, they have all, except the *Legations*, been completely translated into English. And many first-rate books, not to mention hundreds of articles, have been dedicated to expounding them. But even so, Machiavelli's writing remains deeply rooted in the historical and cultural soil of a long-forgotten era. Unless you're willing to familiarize yourself with the arcana of sixteenth-century Florence, Italy, and Europe, you'll have a hard time appreciating much of his best work. The one exception is his scintillating *Mandragola*. Almost universally recognized as the greatest comedy of the Italian Renaissance, and believed by many to be the best comedy in any language not written by Shakespeare, the play remains as popular and accessible as it was in its own time.

Still, there can be no doubt of the timeliness of Machiavelli's example of civic engagement. His sensitivity to the intoxicating influence of power is borne out by the "fascist shift" inaugurated by our own present leaders.[1] Where Machiavelli's countrymen feared the imperial ambitions of other states, our menace comes from within, from executives who make decisions not pragmatically but ideologically, not legally but in blatant violation of the Constitution, and not publicly but behind closed doors. During the Vietnam War, the comic strip character Pogo chided us, "We have met the enemy, and they are us." As I write these words in 2008, the catchwords of our public discourse are *Abu Ghraib*, *Guantanamo*, and *extraordinary rendition*, while lawsuits and Congressional hearings probe an American president's self-proclaimed authority to spy on U.S. citizens in the name of "homeland security." If Machiavelli matters to contemporary Americans, it is at least partly due to his reminder that the first duty of a citizen in a republic is to be informed about the facts underlying any political decision and to channel that information to the skeptical exchange of opinion in the public marketplace of political discourse.

The book's plan is fairly straightforward. Chapter 1 sketches the historical context in which Machiavelli worked and wrote. After tracing the evolution of the Florentine Republic to its fall in 1512, I review Machiavelli's main activities during his fourteen-year tenure in the Soderini Republic and then his mostly writerly endeavors in the remaining fifteen years of his life following its fall. Readers more interested in

Machiavelli's thought than in his work might want to skip this chapter and/or return to it later. Chapter 2 outlines Machiavelli's practical reportage as his city's interpreter, recording first the practical substance of his dispatches, then his analyses of current events, and finally his "metadiscourses" or reflections on his own role. In Chapter 3, I take up the question of Machiavelli's political philosophy, concentrating on his three major works: *The Prince*, the *Discourses*, and the *Florentine Histories*. Chapters 4 and 5 focus on two key terms in Machiavelli's take on the citizen in the world: *virtù*, especially as it denotes civic virtue, in Chapter 4; and *fortuna*, in the sense of external challenges to that virtue, in Chapter 5. Finally, Chapter 6 attempts to assess Machiavelli's stature as a writer, taking account of the full range of his poetic and dramatic writing, as well as his view of himself as poet and writer. A brief concluding chapter directly takes up the titular question of the book. Again, to get a glimpse of where all this is leading with respect to our own times, the reader may want to sneak a look at this part before plunging into the body of the text.

In lieu of a formal acknowledgment, I would like to thank Jennifer Bernard for combing through the manuscript with her keen writer's eye and excising dozens of errors and infelicities, and Artis Bernard for reading it through not once but twice! I also want to thank Ray Waddington, the editor of this series, for kindly inviting me to write the book, as well as my editor, Brian Foster, for his encouragement and patience.

I should emphasize at the outset that this book is not for specialists. Though no doubt my opinions on matters Machiavellian will differ from, and of course owe much to, those of scholars who have studied his life and works, I do not intend here to offer a new interpretation of them or to alter the consensus, such as it is, on their implications. My sole aim is to try to persuade my readers that Machiavelli does indeed matter to those of us who would accept the burden of democratic citizenship. For that reason, besides my formal dedication, I wish to dedicate the book to my fellow grassroots activists in the Maine People's Alliance—*my* Second Chancery! At the risk of omitting others who belong here, I write in the hope of sharing my debt to and inspiration by Machiavelli with Adam, Ali, Amy, Andre, Artis, Ashley, Ben, Billy, David, Donna, Greg, JB, Jacquie, Jay, Jenny, Jesse, Josh, Judy, Kate B., Kate W., Kevin, Mal, Milt, Nikki, Paul, Pete, Peter, Rufus, Sara, Seth, Steve, Sue, Tammy, Wells, and many more with whom I've been privileged to occupy the trenches in the battle to strengthen the democratic fabric of my adoptive state.

If they or other readers of this book come to recognize in Machiavelli a guardian spirit of the communal values we cherish, I'll be content.

CHAPTER 1

INTRODUCTION: MACHIAVELLI IN HIS TIME

Niccolò Machiavelli, the man destined to be a seminal figure for those living in a democracy for centuries to come, was born in Florence on May 3, 1469, and baptized on May 4 in the baptistery at San Giovanni. His father, Bernardo di Niccolò di Buoninsegna, belonged to an impoverished branch of the family that had occupied high offices in the city government.[1] Little is known of his early life; he began learning Latin grammar from one Maestro Matteo in 1476, and his mother died some twenty years later. Then in 1498, at the exact midpoint of his life—*nel mezzo del cammin di sua vita*, to paraphrase Dante—and five days after the execution of the firebrand Dominican friar Savonarola, he was appointed by the Florentine council as second chancellor of the republic, with a special responsibility for military affairs. In that post for the remaining fourteen years of the republic, he lived the active political life of a citizen. During these critical years he worked in close association with Piero Soderini, who in 1502 was granted a lifetime appointment as gonfalonier or standard-bearer, the highest magistrate in medieval Italian city-states.

The author of *The Prince*, then, that scandalous treatise on authoritarian rule, was a dyed-in-the-wool republican. Hence the appropriate context in which to view Machiavelli's political career is the Florentine Republic itself. From its origins in the twelfth century until its fall in 1512, the storied mercantile commune on the banks of the Arno River furnishes a compelling chapter in the emergence of modern Europe out of the ruins of the Islamic Middle Ages. Whereas southern Italy remained feudal well into the early modern period, the cities and towns of the north were, almost from the outset, dominated by commerce. Even in the so-called Dark Ages urban life under the Romans was never completely wiped out on the peninsula, especially north of Rome. In Venice, trade, and in Milan, finance, took hold and gradually increased from the eleventh century on. In Tuscany, the urban revival centered in protective associations of merchant venturers, guilds of craftsmen, and executive committees of distinguished citizens known first as "good men" and later, in homage to ancient Rome, "consuls."[2]

Prime among the Tuscan cities was Florence. The first authoritative reference to consuls dates from 1138, and the earliest surviving record of a merchant guild from 1182. In both cases, the institution itself is undoubtedly older. The guilds or *arti* were the city's greatest source of strength, though membership probably was never more than 3,000 to 4,000 out of a total population of 100,000 enrolled in some twenty-one guilds. From the twelfth to the early fifteenth centuries, the guilds surmounted recurring tensions—including periodic armed conflict—both among themselves and with the much larger proletariat, to maintain a degree of internal liberty and a wavering prosperity.

In the fifteenth century, republicanism gave way to oligarchic rule, eventually under the Medici. This regime virtually excluded the "people." Though theoretically limited by the will of the populace, power resided in the Signoria, whose members were elected from a political class of about 2,000 out of about 10,000 males over the age of twenty-five.[3] These domestic changes are inseparable from external events. The city's military victory over Milan in 1402 triggered a rise in civic pride, expressed in the myths of "humanist" culture. From the beginning, political power in Florence had been concentrated in a tight fraternity of rich merchant families. This order was firmly established when a pro-Medici government took power. The Medici hegemony can be traced to the family's dominance, under Giovanni di Bicci (d. 1419) and his son Cosimo, over the rival Albizzis following the war with Lucca in 1433. A year later, Cosimo was recalled from exile, launching over half a century of effective Medici rule in the nominal republic.

Throughout his thirty-year reign, Cosimo kept a low profile, quietly building a family dynasty while allowing himself to be appointed gonfalonier, or magistrate, only in 1435, 1439, and 1445. His power was secured with the death of Rinaldo degli Albizzi in 1442. He strategically married the Contessina Bardi, who bore him two sons, Giovanni and Piero. While Giovanni's only son died young, and Giovanni died in 1463, Piero and his offspring played a prominent role in both the family's and the city's fortunes, as we will see. As always, the former depended in great part on the latter. In the shifting power struggle for preeminence on the peninsula, in 1450 Francesco Sforza had become the first Duke of Milan. Cosimo supported Milan and its duke against the seemingly greater threat of Venice, until that threat was weakened by the Turks' capture of Constantinople in 1453. Dissension arising from the peace of Lodi between Milan and Venice in 1454 led to a restoration of elections, as well as to additional reforms four years later.

Following Cosimo's death in 1464, power in Florence devolved to his surviving son, Piero. Like his father, Piero married within the upper echelons of Florentine commercial society; in due course, Lucrezia Tornabuoni bore him two sons, Lorenzo (b. 1449) and Giuliano, as well as three daughters. Piero outlived his father by only five years. Having surmounted more trouble with the Sforza and an internal conspiracy, he died in 1469, six months after Lorenzo's marriage to Clarice Orsini, and the year of Machiavelli's birth. Piero's brief reign figures in history as a minor parenthesis between the stealth reign of Cosimo, also known as the "father of his country," and the more glittering one of his "magnificent" son, Lorenzo.

Lorenzo's court was impressive. Culturally, it encompassed the Neoplatonic flights of Marsilio Ficino, the classical scholarship of Poliziano, and the visual splendors of Botticelli. Put another way, it ran the gamut from the "serene perfection of Leonardo," to the "tragic realism of Machiavelli," the "creative imagination of Michelangelo" and the "compulsive rantings of Savonarola."[4] Like his father and grandfather, Lorenzo presided over this scene as an "under-cover ruler," his soubriquet "*Il Magnifico*" being a typical courtesy title of the time. The early years of his reign were relatively uneventful, as he sought to maintain peace on the peninsula through alliances with Milan and Naples. Inexorably, however, relations with the Church worsened when Pope Sixtus IV annexed Imola in 1474, prompting Lorenzo to abandon his Milan-Naples alliance against Venice for a Milan-Venice pact against Naples, now allied with the Pope.

Meanwhile, things at home took a dark turn, ultimately reversed by a combination of Lorenzo's luck and his skills. In 1478, Girolamo

Riario organized the so-called Pazzi Conspiracy in Florence. On April 26 of that year, assassins boldly attacked the Medici brothers at the cathedral of Santa Maria del Fiore, better known as the "Duomo," killing Giuliano but allowing the wounded Lorenzo to escape. The following summer, the Pope tried to capitalize on the resulting instability by launching a war throughout Italy. This conflict ended in 1480 when Lorenzo risked capture in Naples to achieve a peace treaty. When the Turks seized Otranto in August, the Pope grudgingly signed on to a reconciliation with Florence.

In the decade or so remaining to him, Lorenzo sought to restore stability both in Italy and at home. Yet despite his efforts to keep the Pope from turning Rome into a fifth major Italian state, after Sixtus died in 1484, Innocent VIII maintained the threat of a peninsular war by attacking Naples. In the decade that followed, Lorenzo married his daughter Maddelena to the new Pope's son, and saw his own seventeen-year-old son Giovanni, the future Leo X, installed as a cardinal. Soon thereafter, Lorenzo retreated to his villa at Careggi, where he died in April 1492. Two years later, Piero was driven out of office. The next eighteen years saw the last heroic struggle of the Florentine Republic to ward off Medici domination. Two weeks after Piero's banishment, as the French king Charles VIII was staging his triumphal entry into Florence on November 17, 1494, the republic was renewed. Florence would pay the price of this stubborn loyalty to France when the treaty of Cateau-Cambrésis cemented Spanish conquest of the peninsula in 1559.

The glory days of the restored republic were to be short-lived. Reveling in their victory, the republicans honed their civic skills under the new regime led by Savonarola, who dominated the city from 1494 to 1498.[5] After his fall, they continued to do so for the fourteen years of the Soderini republic, during which time the distrusted Medici remained in exile. As we have seen, at this time Machiavelli himself was installed as second chancellor, a position he retained to the end, and four years later his friend Piero Soderini was made the republic's first gonfalonier for life. His, and the republic's, nemesis was as always imperial Spain. When in 1510 Pope Julius II rallied the peninsula against the foreign invaders, Florence once again cast its lot with France. The Spanish victory at Ravenna triggered Cardinal Giovanni de' Medici's installation as ruler of Florence in 1512. On the death of

Pope Julius, Giovanni was elected Leo X and his brother Giuliano was installed in Florence, to be succeeded on his death in 1516 by Piero II's son Lorenzo, later Duke of Urbino. When Lorenzo died in 1519, he was succeeded by Cardinal Giulio de' Medici, the illegitimate son of Giuliano, who in 1523 was elected Pope Clement VII.

Machiavelli's part in these events was neither spectacular nor negligible. In his role as second chancellor, his duties dealt mainly with correspondence regarding the administration of Florence's territories. But he also functioned as one of the six secretaries to the first chancellor and as such was asked to serve the Ten of War, who were also responsible for the republic's foreign and diplomatic relations. In this capacity, he was frequently asked to travel abroad, acting as secretary to the Ten's ambassadors and helping to file reports on foreign affairs.

Throughout his thirties, then, Machiavelli was basically a foot soldier for the republic, revered as a boon companion by his colleagues in the chancery, but also frequently chosen by the Council to take part in crucial negotiations abroad. On these missions, because of his relatively modest social status, Machiavelli usually accompanied and advised a member of the Florentine aristocracy who was nominally the key player. As an "envoy," not ambassador, his job on such missions was not to negotiate, but to observe and report back to the Council or Signoria in official legations. He also communicated with his friends and patrons in private correspondence.[6] When he wasn't performing diplomatic tasks, his chief preoccupation was organizing local militia. Convinced that the key to preserving liberty was to replace Florence's traditional reliance on mercenaries with a citizen army, Machiavelli devoted much of his energy in Florence to selling this idea to his countrymen and much of his time in the countryside to enlisting and training troops. While this chapter will focus on his diplomatic missions, there is little doubt that if asked, Machiavelli would have said that his most important work was military preparation.

Machiavelli's first five years in the chancery culminated in his, and Florence's, wary relations with Cesare Borgia, the charismatic military champion of his father, the Pope. Machiavelli spent much of this period either at the court of Duke Valentino, as Borgia preferred to be called, or negotiating directly or indirectly with King Louis XII of France to help check the Duke's expanding influence, as well as to help Florence regain its lost territories around Pisa. Before his close association with Duke Valentino began, however, he made several other diplomatic junkets: to Caterina Sforza, Countess of Imoli and Forlì, in 1499; and to Georges d'Amboise, Cardinal of Rouen, and Louis XII a year later.[7] Having returned to Florence in January 1501, the next month Machiavelli was in Carmignano dealing with a rebellion in Pistoia; the rest of the year he spent tracking the Duke's movements in the Romagna.

At this time, Machiavelli initiated nearly a year of intense relations with Duke Valentino, richly recorded in his letters and, less directly, in *The Prince*. After the briefest of respites, during which he married Marietta, the daughter of Luigi Corsini, in June 1502, he met with the duke at Urbino. There, Valentino warned Florence of the consequences of its loyalty to France, casting himself not as a tyrant but as a conqueror of tyrants. In October, Machiavelli reencountered the duke at Imola, where he professed his faith in the Florentine Republic. On the following day, the duke called him back to offer an alliance with Florence, which Machiavelli duly reported to the Ten, along with his suspicions of the duke's treachery.

Remaining at court until the end of the year, Machiavelli reported every few days on his continuing conversations with Valentino.[8] At this time, he witnessed firsthand the dramatic events at Cesena recorded in Chapter 7 of *The Prince*: the public retribution bestowed on Ramiro Lorqua in the public square of Cesena on December 26, and the assassination of various Orsini and Vitelli five days later at Senigallia. Though he could hardly have suspected it, in this period of relentless negotiation Machiavelli was witnessing the swan song of Cesare Borgia. On returning to Florence a few weeks later, he wrote several reports on matters in Pistoia and Pisa as well as the *Description of the Method Used by Duke Valentino in Killing Vitellozzi Vitelli, Oliverotto da Fermo*. He had barely completed a trip to Siena when news arrived in August of the death of Pope Alexander VI, the one contingency capable of thwarting the duke's ambitions and precipitating his fall from power.

The death of the Pope and waning of his son prompted a period of instability in Italy. For Machiavelli, despite his continuing missions abroad, it meant redirecting his energies to the war with Pisa and his efforts to recruit a citizen army. The Pisan adventure might have ended in 1505 had not the Florentine army, fresh from a major victory at San Vincenzo in August, failed to breach the Pisan walls. For the next four years, Machiavelli tirelessly pursued this enterprise. In the first half of 1506, he sought and trained peasant conscripts, reviewing his recruits in February in the Piazza della Signoria. Finally, after several months of military and diplomatic maneuvering, in which Machiavelli played a central part, on June 4, 1509, Pisa surrendered. Four days later, culminating a fifteen-year conflict, the Florentine forces, with Machiavelli in their ranks, entered the city.

In the meantime, Machiavelli maintained a brisk diplomatic schedule, visiting several of the major courts of Europe from 1503 to 1509. In October 1503, following the death of Pius III, he was sent by the Ten to Rome to observe the ensuing Conclave, at which Giuliano delle Rovere was elected as Julius II in early November. Duke Valentino was also in Rome for these events, and Machiavelli met with him to hear his complaints at the Florentines' refusal of his request for a safe conduct for his troops on their way to Romagna. Assured of the Pope's mistrust of the duke, Machiavelli advised the Ten to ignore his ambassador even though his army was counting on their safe conduct.[9] A few days later, he was with the Pope when he learned of the duke's capture. His mission in Rome had been accomplished, the city was experiencing a plague, and he had learned of the birth of a son, Bernardo. Nevertheless, despite repeated orders from the Ten, Machiavelli resisted leaving Rome. Only after more than a month there did he reluctantly return to Florence, in December 1503.

With one major exception, Machiavelli's remaining diplomatic assignments at this time were in Italy. The exception came in late January and February 1504, when he was sent with the Florentine ambassador Niccolò Valori to Lyons, where the two Niccolòs failed to deflect the French from concluding a truce with Spain. Back in Florence, toward the end of October he completed the first *Decennale*, a 550-line poem on events in Italy during the decade beginning with the descent of Charles VIII in 1494. The following April saw him haggling with Giampaolo Baglioni, lord of Perugia, at Castiglione del Lago over the latter's abandonment of his commission to defend Florence against a hostile coalition. In May, Machiavelli vainly sought help against this plot from the Marquis of Mantua, and in July from Pandolfo Petrucci of Siena.

Apart from his military activities, the next three years were a relatively light period. The second half of 1506—as we have seen, the first half was given to military efforts—was spent mostly with the Pope.

Julius had asked the Florentines to aid him in his expedition against the Bentivoglio of Bologna. Reluctant to do so, they sent Machiavelli to play for time. Catching up with the papal court, he stayed with it until it arrived at Perugia. There, stunned by the Pope's "rashness" and Giampaolo's "cowardice," Machiavelli watched Julius face down the Baglioni by boldly entering the city in advance of his troops, an episode he duly recorded in the *Discourses*, I.27. Possibly inspired by this event, he penned his famous *Ghiribizzi* or "fantasies" (L. 121, September 13–21, 1506), in which he marvels at the diverse consequences of the same acts under different circumstances.[10]

Pope Julius stayed in Perugia through September and then moved on to Cesena to await French aid. At Forlì in October, he issued a bull against Bentivoglio, telling Machiavelli that he was ready to use Marcantonio Colonna and his men against his enemy. Convinced that Julius was a potential liberator and uniter of Italy, Machiavelli embraced his cause with relish. At Imola, he explained to the Bolognese ambassadors why the Florentines were marching with the Pope. He was still there when Julius accepted Bologna's surrender. By the time he made his solemn entry into the city in November, Machiavelli was back in Florence, where he wrote the *Discourse on the Military Organization of the State of Florence*. In December, the Nine Officials of the Ordinance and Militia were installed, with Machiavelli as its chancellor. He could now add "Secretary of the Nine" to his titles of "Chancellor of the Second Chancery" and "Secretary of the Ten."

Machiavelli's next assignments all reflected Florentine fears of aggressive action by the Emperor Maximilian. Reviving echoes of the Holy Roman Empire, Maximilian had secured promises of troops and money to invade Italy, drive the French king out of Lombardy, and receive the imperial crown at Rome. In Florence, Soderini wanted to send Machiavelli to keep an eye on Maximilian, but once again the opposition demanded an envoy with greater social standing. Or perhaps the real reason for his non-appointment was his difficult and controversial attitude, as reflected in his letters' blend of stinginess with information and uninvited (and unappreciated) opinions.[11] In any event, in June, Francesco Vettori undertook the commission. But Machiavelli was to have his own go at German affairs, in a series of assignments that resulted in publishing, after his return to Florence in 1508, his *Report on the State of Germany*, revised and reissued in 1512.

This phase of Machiavelli's diplomacy got under way late in the summer of 1507. In August, the Pope's legate to Maximilian, Cardinal Carvajal, passed through Florence, and the Ten commissioned their secretary to scout him out, which he did in letters from Siena and San Quirico d'Orcia. Meanwhile, unhappy with Vettori as their representative at the imperial court, the gonfalonier got the Ten to send Machiavelli after him to do what he could to win, or buy, Maximilian's favor. In January 1508, he joined Vettori at Bolzano, initiating a long and fruitful friendship between the two men. There, Machiavelli began his negotiations with the emperor, impressing him with his hard-nosed diplomatic skill. For his part, Maximilian, biding his time, eventually demanded an immediate loan of 25,000 ducats plus a tribute to be negotiated when he reached the Po River. Predictably, the tight-fisted Florentines refused. Moving to Innsbruck, then back to Bolzano, Vettori and Machiavelli returned to Trent in March to hear the emperor's final request for 60,000 ducats in three quick installments.

Even as these diplomatic efforts were unfolding, Machiavelli's German mission was winding down. While the Florentines temporized and the emperor's grandiose plans were hobbled by defeat at the hands of the Venetians, Machiavelli, who was suffering from gallstones, parted with Vettori at Trent in June, ending his six-month tour in Germany. He reached Florence just in time for the final showdown with Pisa, launched in August and consummated, as we have seen, less than a year later. Following the Pisan surrender in mid-November 1509, Machiavelli was sent to Mantua to hand over an installment of the 40,000-ducat tribute the Florentines had finally agreed to pay the emperor. Learning that Vicenza had rebelled and expelled the imperial garrison, he rushed to Verona to await Maximilian, managing to get through just before the roads were cut. Here he wrote the second *Decennale*, as well as the famous description of his encounter with an aging crone in a local brothel (L. 178, December 8, 1509). Returning to Mantua, he received permission to go home and returned to Florence in January 1510.

During the final years of the Soderini Republic, Machiavelli's activities again oscillated between efforts to improve his city's military readiness and diplomatic undertakings to protect it in the looming international crisis. The latter centered on the struggle between France and Spain for dominance of the peninsula, which only seemed to be settled in the Battle of Ravenna, won inconclusively by the French in April 1512. Throughout the winter of 1510–1511, Machiavelli was raising troops in the Tuscan countryside. In February 1512, he organized a parade in the Piazza della Signoria, leading to the passage in March of a bill providing for a mounted militia. From Pisa, where he was reorganizing the garrison of the citadel, he was sent to Siena to offer condolences for the death of Pandolfo Petrucci. After supervising the organization of the Pisan cavalry in June, Machiavelli returned to Florence. As the new Holy League of the Pope, Venice, Ferrara, and Spain prepared to restore Medici rule in Florence, July and August found him once again raising troops, this time in the Mugello. At this critical moment, on August 24, Machiavelli was precipitously recalled to Florence to help prepare to defend the city against the Spanish troops reported to be on their way to Rome.

On the diplomatic front, Machiavelli's efforts at this time centered in France. With Pope Julius leading the resistance against the French threat to Venice, the Florentines sent Machiavelli in 1510 to treat with their long-time allies. While he was with the French court at Blois, he heard Louis XII's demands that Florence actively support him against the Pope. Following a long discussion with the French ambassador Robertet (or Rubertet), Machiavelli wrote the Ten to warn them that no neutrality was possible for Florence. Suffering now from the whooping cough, he asked permission to return to Florence, finally arriving home in October. The next four months, as we have seen, found him engaged with military matters.

As for the Pope, in a rapid reversal of his fortunes at the beginning of 1511, he had been defeated at Ferrara, lost Bologna, and withdrawn to Rimini. Then, when Louis XII withdrew instead of pushing his advantage, the Florentines, fearing the Pope's retribution, sent Machiavelli to ward him off. Leaving for France in September, at Blois he again appeared before King Louis, along with the ambassador who had replaced him the year before, Roberto Acciaiuoli, the same day the Pope issued an interdict against Florence. After trying unsuccessfully to persuade the king against war, he received permission from the Ten to return once more to Florence, arriving there in early November, only to find the city filled with rumors and omens of impending catastrophe. Far from immune to such superstitions himself, on November 22, 1511, Machiavelli made his first will.

His forebodings were more than vindicated in the fateful year that followed. It began auspiciously enough with Machiavelli conveying his instructions to Francesco Guicciardini, the Florentine ambassador to the King of Aragon. But despite the defensive preparations he supervised throughout the year, doom was descending on the Florentines. In August 1512, the Spaniards sacked Prato; in September, Soderini was ousted, the Medici returned as private citizens, and Giovanni Ridolfi was elected gonfalonier. Later in the month, the Nine in charge of militia were dismissed, Soderini was banished, the Great Council was abolished, and Ridolfi was forced to resign, effectively restoring Medici rule. In these circumstances, Machiavelli's own security was clearly imperiled. In November, he was dismissed as second chancellor and secretary to the Ten and confined in Florentine territory for one year; on November 17, he began his exile on his farm in Sant' Andrea in Percussina. This presumably temporary banishment was interrupted in February and March 1513. Falsely associated with an anti-Medici conspiracy, Machiavelli was recalled to Florence, where he was imprisoned, subjected to six "drops" on the rope, and, following the death of Julius and election of Leo X on March 11, released from prison after twenty-two days and allowed to return to Sant' Andrea.

Such were Machiavelli's years as a nonpartisan civil servant to the Florentine republic. As we will see in the next chapter, in his secretarial function, Machiavelli wrote in the role and style of a good humanist. As a diplomat, his forty missions in fourteen years in the chancery fall within an emerging fifteenth-century tradition, though he was diplomatically the most active of the chancery secretaries in this period. As a bureaucrat, he represented the new separation of the legal and political sectors of government. Elected to the chancery because he *wasn't* political, his hatred for the aristocrats who destroyed the Soderini Republic was offset by his impartiality on his imperial legation of 1508 and his mission to the French court in 1510, his acquaintance with Soderini opponents as well as supporters, and even the nature of his relations with Piero Soderini himself. Indeed, Machiavelli may have shared Soderini's own nonpartisan bias, as suggested by the theme of "political harmony" in his writings before 1512 and continued in those after Soderini's fall.[12]

The fourteen years remaining to Machiavelli virtually constitute his life as a writer—not that he hadn't written prolifically during his active period. But, however grudgingly, in the years of his exile from public life, Machiavelli became increasingly absorbed in his literary efforts, eventually even defining himself as "Niccolò Machiavelli, *istorico, comico e tragico*" (L. 300, after October 21, 1525). Applying this terminology loosely to his output, we can identify two distinct phases: "literary" (comic and tragic) and historiographical.[13] In the first of these periods, which includes *The Prince*, the *Discourses*, *Mandragola*, *The Golden Ass*, and *Belfagor*, as well as much of his incidental poetry, his writing served as either an outlet for his frustration or an instrument in his campaign to reclaim his political vocation. The second period, comprising *The Art of War*, possibly the *Life of Castruccio Castracani*, and the *Florentine Histories*, earned him permanent status as a man of letters.

Nevertheless, almost from the day of his release from prison, Machiavelli sought to reassert himself as an active player on the new Medici stage. Writing in mid-March from Florence, he asked his friend Vettori in Rome to keep his name before the Pope (L. 204, March 13, 1513). A few days later, even while proclaiming a stoical resignation, he hoped the Medici would "see fit not to leave me lying on the ground" (L. 206, March 18, 1513). Subsequent letters to Vettori show Machiavelli angling for employment in Rome if not in Florence, where he was more suspect (L. 210, April 16, 1513). His literary texts themselves seem to reinforce these efforts. The third and most pious of the generally impious Carnival Songs may have been written at this time; two of his pleading sonnets to the current ruler in Florence, "To Giuliano di Lorenzo de' Medici" and "To the Same," certainly were. Other letters—especially to Vettori, with whom Machiavelli's mainly epistolary friendship was cemented during the months following his release from prison—are more resigned. Yet from the end of 1513 comes perhaps his most famous letter, in which he reveals that he has been writing *The Prince* and is thinking of offering it to Giuliano (L. 224, December 10, 1513).

In fact, the hope of finding employment was never far from Machiavelli's thoughts. Even the account of his life in retirement ends with hope that the Medici will engage his services. And when Vettori failed to reply to this hint, he followed up with another letter asking if he should come to Rome (L. 225, December 19, 1513). Vettori's reply to these appeals cannot have been very encouraging. He responded to the proposed visit by noting that there was nothing "suitable" for Machiavelli to do there, putting him off with a vague allusion to Cardinal Giulio's being named as a legate to France (L. 226, December 24, 1513). Undiscouraged, Machiavelli kept working on *The Prince*, some chapters of which Vettori acknowledged having read, though he reserved judgment until he had read the work in its entirety (L. 228, January 18, 1514).[14] Despite this lukewarm response, in January 1514, after eight months in the country, Machiavelli moved with his family back to Florence. He was full of hope and brought with him notebooks containing parts of the *Discourses* and *The Prince*.

Though rich in literary achievements, the period that followed was disappointing to Machiavelli's hopes for employment. Whiling away his days at the shop of his friend Donato del Corno and his evenings at the house of the courtesan Riccia, he poured his energy into his correspondence with Vettori, who had now been in Rome as ambassador for two years.[15] Vettori's letter quashing any hope of employment in Rome is lost, but Machiavelli's response to it reveals the intensity of his disappointment. It runs the gamut from devastation—"So I am going to stay just as I am amid my lice"—to resignation—he has given up "thoughts about matters great and grave" and is reading about deeds ancient or modern—to distraction: he has fallen in love with one of his country neighbors (L. 236, June 10, 1514, and 238, August 3, 1514).

Machiavelli's efforts to lose himself in affairs of the heart were soon thwarted. In December 1514, his pledge never to discuss politics again was challenged when Vettori posed him a strategic problem regarding the current situation in Europe, his answer to which was sure to be read by the Pope. Machiavelli responded with gusto and at great length, and then launched another appeal for employment (L. 241, December 10, 1514). Vettori reported that both letters had been seen by the Pope, who, though impressed, had given him nothing but words (L. 245, December 30, 1514). Machiavelli's brother Paolo was more upbeat. Returning to Florence from Rome in late December, he assured Machiavelli that both of them would soon have a role in a new state the Pope was carving out in the north. By the end of January 1515, Machiavelli was conveying advice to Giuliano through Paolo on how to rule the new state. Unbeknownst to him, however, even as these proposals were circulating, Machiavelli's old adversary Piero

Ardinghelli, the papal secretary, wrote to Giuliano advising him to avoid him like the plague.[16]

Little is recorded of Machiavelli in the turbulent years that follow, but it is clear that he continued to cultivate his muse. In 1515, Louis XII died and was succeeded by the belligerent François I, who, coveting Milan, entered Italy and defeated the Swiss at Marignano. Meanwhile, in Florence the ill and ineffective Giuliano, destined to die the following year, was replaced by the young Lorenzo, who captured Urbino for the Pope in June 1516 and became its duke four months later. Well aware of these events, Machiavelli altered the dedication of *The Prince* from Giuliano to Lorenzo. The attempt was notoriously unsuccessful—Lorenzo is said to have preferred the gift of a pair of coursing dogs—and in February 1516, Machiavelli wrote to his nephew Vernacci that he was "useless" to himself, his family, and his friends (L. 250, February 15, 1516). By 1517, he was once again living on his farm, sometimes going for a month at a time "without thinking of myself" (L. 252, June 8, 1517). Yet, in this fallow time he worked on *The Golden Ass*, took part in literary and philosophical discussions in the Orti Oricellari, resumed work on the *Discourses*, and wrote his comic masterpiece, *Mandragola*.[17]

Lorenzo died in 1519, and was succeeded by Cardinal Giulio de' Medici, the future Pope Clement VII. For Machiavelli, these events signaled a long-awaited reversal of fortune and ushered in the era of "Niccolò Machiavelli *storico*." The cardinal received him in March and perhaps even encouraged him to complete the *Art of War*. His prospects improved even further when he learned that the new Pope was thinking of producing *Mandragola* in Rome the following year and commissioning a new writing project. During a prolonged business trip to Lucca, Machiavelli wrote the *Life of Castruccio Castracani*, possibly as an audition piece for the role of official historian of the Florentine Republic. If so, the ploy worked. Aided by friends backed by Cardinal Giulio, in November he was hired by university officials to serve for two years in that capacity and was commissioned by the cardinal himself to write a *Discourse on Florentine affairs after the death of Lorenzo*, which was presented to the Pope in 1520.

Machiavelli's remaining years were devoted mainly to historiography. Following a commission in 1521 to the Minor Friars at Capri, he returned to the country to resume his writing. From this safe haven he was content to follow at a distance Pope Leo's shift of allegiance in May from France to the Hapsburg Empire. The Pope's sudden death and the election of Adrian VI in January 1522 brought the frustrated Cardinal Giulio back to Florence, where Machiavelli offered advice on governing by writing *A Discourse on Remodeling the Government of Florence*, in which he slyly repeated his proposal to revive the popular state, to be governed by the Medici during his lifetime and rendered free thereafter. Giulio may have actually been considering this plan when, in June, yet another anti-Medici conspiracy was uncovered, this one involving some of the Orti Oricellari literati. Machiavelli's former boss, Piero Soderini, died a few days after the plot's discovery—prompting a libelous epitaph in which Machiavelli consigns him to a special limbo of fools—but his brother, the cardinal, was imprisoned. Machiavelli was still in the country when he learned of the death of Adrian VI in September and the election of Giulio de' Medici as Clement VII in November 1523. There he made his second and final will. By this time, he had probably reached the point in his history of Florence where he was to discuss the actions of the new Pope's uncle, Lorenzo.

With a few exceptions, Machiavelli's final activities were not political, but literary and amatory. Early in 1524, gourmandizing at the suburban home of the rich plebian Fornaccio, he began an affair with the charming young actress and singer "Barbera," whose real name was probably Barbara Raffacani Salutati. For her he added songs for a projected revival of *Mandragola* that never came off, and by her he was inspired to write *Clizia*, with its self-ironic portrayal of an aging lover, composed hastily for presentation at a party at Fornaccio's in January 1525.[18] In May of that year, Machiavelli decided to go to Rome to present Clement the *Histories*. There he also succeeded at last in selling his idea for a national militia to the Pope and his advisers, who sent him at once to Faenza with an urgent papal brief urging his old friend Guicciardini, now president of Romagna, to attend to Machiavelli and send back his verdict. Forewarned of the mission, Guicciardini received the proposal coldly, and when no decision was forthcoming in more than a month, Machiavelli returned to Florence, launching a correspondence with his now much closer friend and resuming his dalliance with Barbera.

What should have been the mellow twilight of his career as retired diplomat-turned-successful author was shadowed by the relentless unfolding of the Italian tragedy. Even as Machiavelli was revising *Mandragola* for the proposed Faenza production in February 1526, Guicciardini himself was preparing for a secret mission in Rome to help bring about the Pope's proposed Italian league with Venice and France. Though the Faenza revival, as Guicciardini knew, would never come off, the same month saw the play's second smashing revival in Venice. The author himself, meanwhile, was pushing ahead with his *Histories*.

In April, on orders from the Pope, Machiavelli submitted a report about the defense of Florence that earned him a call to Rome and, on his return, election as secretary and quartermaster, his last official post in Florence. In May, François I repudiated the Treaty of Madrid and formed the League of Cognac, allying himself with the Pope, Milan, Venice, and Florence against Charles V. Machiavelli was with the League's army in Milan, where he spent time with the charismatic Giovanni de' Medici, popularly known as Giovanni delle Bande Nere.[19] Having assisted in the siege of Cremona, in September he rejoined the army in time to witness the capitulation of Milan. This triumph was tempered by the news that the Pope had foolishly dismissed his troops, leaving him vulnerable to an attack by the forces of the Colonna that forced him to take refuge in the Castel Sant' Angelo—a harbinger of the greater catastrophe soon to come.

The curtain would fall on Italy nine months later and on Machiavelli less than a month thereafter. When the Pope accepted a four-month truce, Guicciardini withdrew his troops to Piacenza, where he and Machiavelli joined them in October. With nothing to do there, Machiavelli returned to Florence, only to receive another commission to go to Modena. By the end of November, Giovanni delle Bande Nere was dead. On the day he died, Machiavelli set off, reaching Modena in early December and informing the allies that Florence had little defense remaining against a Spanish attack. He returned to Florence a few days later, but within two months was sent again to Guicciardini to report that the Imperial forces were about to sack both Florence and Rome. After a month in Bologna, in April he went to Imola to arrange billets for the papal troops before returning to Florence.

The story ends with true Machiavellian irony. In early May, the Imperial troops bypassed the city, whose citizens rose up against the Medici in what came to be known as "the Friday tumult." Machiavelli joined Guicciardini in pursuit of the Spaniards, arriving in Orvieto in time to hear of the infamous Sack of Rome on May 6. From there he was sent to Civitavecchia, where he found himself defending the Medici at the very moment that they were being cast out of Florence. By the time he got home in June, he had heard that Francesco Tarugi, first secretary to the now-defunct Eight, had won his old place in the Second Chancery.[20] Falling ill shortly afterwards, and taking some of the famous pills he turned to for all his malaises, he died at home on June 21, 1527, surrounded by friends and joking about his ultimate destination.[21] He was buried the next day in Santa Croce.

CHAPTER 2

THE SECRETARY

Throughout his active life, Machiavelli was engaged in his community, not as a volunteer, but as a professional civil servant. Though variously a chancellor, a recruiter, and frequently (in reality, if not in title) an ambassador, in his years of service to the Florentine Republic, Machiavelli performed primarily as a secretary. To get an idea of what this function entailed, we might consider one of his earliest personal letters (L. 11, probably early October 1499). Here, in only his second year in the chancery, Machiavelli scolds an indiscreet Luccan secretary for abusing his office. In a letter that has found its way into Machiavelli's hands regarding a matter close to his heart, his anonymous addressee has cast "opprobrium" on Florence by criticizing its failure to take Pisa. In doing so, the Luccan, like Machiavelli an "interpreter" (literally "the tongue") of his republic, has not only revealed his malice but, more importantly, demonstrated his ineptitude, both by swallowing whole what he has heard. After defending his city against the charges made, Machiavelli ends by sardonically counseling his correspondent "in brotherly love" to insult more prudently in the future.[1]

That Machiavelli should think of himself in his official function as merely the interpreter of Florence may come as a surprise to readers accustomed to viewing him as a highly original commentator on political behavior. We are dealing here with more than simply his situation before and after his fall from grace. Even in his active days, Machiavelli always drew a line between his duties and responsibilities as an agent of the state and his personal views, carefully distinguishing between the diplomatic conveyance of information and the uncensored, sometimes even wildly fantastic, ruminations of a pleasure-loving man of affairs frequently away from hearth and home. Nor was the more personal side of the equation necessarily inconsequential. In absence, even on state business, one's reputation could soar or plunge on a single bit of gossip, and an ambassador necessarily left his back exposed at home. Therefore, the pull of the personal can be felt in many of Machiavelli's most sober reports. Still, the distinction between reportage and interpretation was crucial, as is minimally displayed in a letter written in June 1506, where a series of curt "dispatches" on the political situation in Europe is followed by a typically Machiavellian analysis couched as the reflections "of the wisest men": for example, "this is how their reasoning goes," "People therefore conclude," "this is how reason would have it," "People also think," "people do not think," "people therefore believe," and so forth (L. 112, June 12, 1506).

The more amiable side of our man comes out especially in his friends' responses. Writing in Latin from Florence to Machiavelli "At the Court of His Most Christian Majesty," Agostino Vespucci regrets the lack of his "amusing, witty, and pleasant conversation" (L. 18, October 20–29, 1500). Two years later, to his friend now "In the Court of the Illustrious Duke of Romagna" Vespucci praises Machiavelli's "spirit ... so eager for riding, wandering, and roaming about," explaining that he is needed in Florence because "[y]ou know the nature of men, their deceptions and secrecy, their rivalries and hatreds" (L. 33, October 14, 1502). In one of the earliest letters from his buddies in the Second Chancery, written during Machiavelli's first mission to France, Biagio Buonaccorsi conveys the general satisfaction with his letters in Florence, detailing the pleasure he and others get from them and acknowledging his envy when he thinks he has been denied one. In a homely postscript, Andrea di Romolo urges Machiavelli to "act like the man of honor you are" by keeping his colleagues informed of his travels (L. 13, August 23, 1500).

Charming as these glimpses into the private man may be, it's Machiavelli the citizen-observer who will occupy us in this chapter. As we have seen, during the attenuated European and Italian crisis precipitated by Charles VIII's descent into Italy, Machiavelli shared his fellow-republicans' struggle to fend off the impending catastrophe. But beyond that, given his official responsibility as his city's "tongue," he was explicitly challenged to keep his colleagues in Florence informed about the ever-evolving continental events he was privileged to observe first-hand. While many of the most crucial moments in this drama were reworked in the pages of *The Prince* and even, more subtly, in his literary texts, it is primarily in his official correspondence with the Ten collected in his voluminous *Legations* that we can best sample the penetration of his observations.[2] Contextualized with his personal correspondence, these texts give the full flavor of Machiavelli as an observer of, and reporter on, the contemporary scene.

Machiavelli's reportage is mainly concentrated in legations and letters generated during a handful of junkets abroad. (I use *abroad* in a Renaissance perspective to denote locales outside of Florence.) Many of his trips to France, Germany, and other parts of Italy are reflected only in letters *to* Machiavelli, though he must have had a major hand in communications made by those he assisted to authorities back home. What follows is a brief summary of his reportage on his visits to France in 1500; to Rome in 1503 and 1506; within Italy in 1505 and 1506; and especially to the mobile court of Cesare Borgia/Duke Valentino in 1502–1503. The bulk of the chapter will then analyze the quality of this reportage, followed by a discussion of his sporadic reflections on his own role as his country's "tongue."

Machiavelli's earliest report from abroad comes from France in the summer and fall of 1500. In August, he records his general observations on Florentine-French relations. Due to Louis XII's stinginess, he observes, France is reluctant to pursue war against Pisa, which the king calls "a mockery." Both the French and the Swiss will require money to go against Pisa: "when force is needed, chalk and reputation are not enough" (*Leg.* August 27, 1500).[3] Four months later he relates to the Ten that, after speaking with the king himself, he has gone to Torcy to persuade Rouen and Robertet to keep Louis committed to the Pisan enterprise.

Between June 1502 and January 1503, Machiavelli reports on several encounters with Cesare Borgia. On June 23, he writes of his and Francesco Soderini's meeting with the duke at Urbino, which the latter had just captured. On their meeting at Imola in early October, he records the "conspiracy of the Magione" (i.e., Vitellozzo Vitelli, Oliverotto da Fermo, Giampaolo Baglioni, and Pandolfo Petrucci), observing that the duke's position is weakened and his posture towards Florence more conciliatory (*Leg.* June 26, 1502). A day or two later, he writes that the duke has shown him a letter from the Pope's French ambassador in which the king and Rouen offer him troops and that he has pointedly repeated his request that Machiavelli ask his superiors to support him. A few days later, he reports that he can get no more out of the duke, who has now been hired as the Florentine general. On October 16, he notes that the duke is sure the king wants Florence to aid him, adding on the 20th his implied threats if Florence continues to demur. On the 27th he lists the duke's possible allies and adversaries. He writes twice on November 8, first to convey the duke's inquires as to what "employment" or "honor" he might expect from Florence as their general, then to repeat at length an appeal made to him by that "friend" first referred to on October 7, in which he urged the profitability of Florence's being the duke's ally. On November 20, he can report that the duke has accepted a "vague alliance" with Florence.

A month later, these reports take a dramatic turn. Machiavelli had provided his Florentine colleagues with a list of Valentino's troop numbers, as acknowledged in a letter from Alamanno Salviati (L. 67, December 23, 1502). In an important dispatch on December 26, having followed the "secretive" duke to Senigallia, where the latter intended to meet and betray the Orsini and Vitelli, he laconically describes how Ramiro Lorqua "was found in two pieces on the public square."[4] On January 1, he relates the subsequent murders of Vitellozzo and Oliverotto, noting that the other (pro-Medici) enemies of Florence, the Orsini, remain free. In this dispatch, he also relays Duke Valentino's request that Florence rejoice in his success, send reinforcements, and detain Guidobaldo da Montefeltro if he comes there.

While less absorbing than his relations with Duke Valentino (and indirectly with his father, Pope Alexander VI), Machiavelli's rare encounters later with Julius II also generated some interesting reports. For the most part, these center on the conclave in which the Pope was elected in 1503 and his bold seizure of Perugia three years later, both of which Machiavelli witnessed firsthand. Sent to Rome following the death of Pius III, he conveyed a number of dispatches between late October and mid-December 1503. Having predicted the election of Giuliano delle Rovere as Pope a day earlier, on November 1 he confirms his succession three times, the last reporting a surprising unanimity, even including the Florentine cardinals. On December 6 he reports on the new Pope's professed amity toward Florence and his efforts to arouse the Curia against Venice.

Though his relations with Machiavelli were less intense than they had been earlier, Duke Valentino was also at court for the election of Julius II, and Machiavelli does not fail to inform the Ten of their encounters. With the chief prop of his power removed by the death of his father, Cesare was now in a precarious position. Even as the Pope kept him waiting—he might need him to ward off the Venetian threat—the duke in turn used Machiavelli to pressure Florence into aiding him in Romagna. On November 6 he reports the duke's furious outburst against Florence for the loss of Imola to Venice. On November 11, he hints that Florence's interests and the Pope's may diverge. In subsequent dispatches, he conveys the news of the duke's departure for Pisa, his refusal to surrender the castle at Forlì to the Pope, his arrest by the latter's men and return in bonds to Rome, his efforts to bargain with the Pope's men, and his ultimate fall from power: "this Duke little by little is slipping into his grave" (*Leg.* December 3, 1503).

Far more compelling is Machiavelli's second encounter with Pope Julius, at Perugia in the fall of 1506. On September 13, having been sent by the Ten to meet the Pope's army on its way to Bologna and temporize with respect to Florentine aid, Machiavelli followed him to Perugia, whence he relates how the Pope single-handedly took Perugia. As Machiavelli describes it, Julius acted alone and with neither premeditation nor hesitation. Leaving his troops in the piazza and at the gates, he boldly entered the city. Julius's victim was its hapless lord, Gianpaolo Baglioni. Though widely known as the typically violent prince of his era, Baglioni comes across here as uncharacteristically passive in the face of the Pope's aggression. Even though the latter was "at his discretion," Gianpaolo refused to do evil to one who was seizing his state, a response that Machiavelli almost wistfully attributes here to "his good nature and humanity."[5]

The last of Machiavelli's reports on the Florence that was is also the saddest. Sometime after September 16, 1512, between the fall of the Soderini Republic in July and Machiavelli's own dismissal in November, he wrote a letter to a "Most Illustrious Lady," possibly Isabella d'Este, in which he relates the catastrophic events of August-September. Reporting a meeting in Mantua in early August where a Medici restoration was negotiated, he then relates how he and his fellow citizens had responded to events, awaiting word of the Spanish army and deciding to send soldiers to Firenzuola but not to deploy them in the open field. When it became clear that the Spanish viceroy wanted to change the government and the army had abandoned their strongholds, Machiavelli's focus shifts to Piero Soderini. At first, the citizens had rallied around him; then, while the Spanish army descended and Soderini procrastinated, the soldiers Machiavelli had recruited turned cowardly and the gonfalonier was forced to depart. The last part of the letter describes how the pro-Medici faction manipulated public opinion—the Medici slogan *"Palle, Palle"* resounding through the piazza—and reinstated "the Magnificent Medici." He ends by laconically claiming to have omitted the more "lamentable" matters (L. 203, after September 16, 1502).[6]

Implied in this reportage is an analytical agenda. While Machiavelli is always acutely aware of his lack of social standing, and therefore often reluctant to go beyond his secretarial function, he is rarely content to stop at the mere relating of facts. An astute observer of men's (and women's) motives, and with a keen sense of the broader political arena in which they are realized, Machiavelli frequently shifts from the reportorial to the analytical mode. These reflections on what he reports range from the definition of his own role to advice to his superiors to reflections on the broader European scene. His powers of analysis are especially on display in his reporting on his encounters with Duke Valentino and Pope Julius II.

Machiavelli is typically reticent about his own role. Nevertheless, in his letters and dispatches he occasionally lets drop comments on what he has done or is doing in the Republic's service. During his trip to France in 1500 to keep the king committed to the Pisan enterprise, he argues that the king is wrong to disapprove of his "children," the Florentines. With Duke Valentino in 1502–1503, he acknowledges that his job is to "temporiz[e]" while "seeking to learn [the duke's] purpose" (*Leg.* October 15, 1502). In a subsequent dispatch, he explains that his overtures to the duke are made by one "speaking always for myself" and not for the Signoria (*Leg.* November 8, 1502). A few weeks later, he reports that he has been working to undermine the credibility of those who have told the duke that Florence is secretly working to oppose him.

Despite this restricted view of his own duties, Machiavelli does not hesitate to advise those at home on the appropriate actions to take. In a dispatch from France in 1500, he warns against the folly of thinking that former beneficial acts will be repeated. "We [Florentines] have often gorged ourselves on empty hopes," he writes; but what happened in the past, when Florence was "vigorous," has now become irrelevant because Florence is perceived to be disunited and weak (*Leg.* August 27, 1500). In his November dispatch from Torcy, he restates the French view of Florence as unreliable because disunited. Machiavelli has advice regarding Duke Valentino and Pope Julius II as well. During his time at Cesare's court in 1502–1503, he implicitly endorses the duke's appeal for help. During his extended stay at the Papal court following the enclave later in 1503, he pragmatically advises the Florentines to expect help from the Pope and Rouen only to save Florence or to protect Romagna.

Occasionally, Machiavelli reflects on the broader European scene. His warnings in 1500 about Florence's deteriorating relations with France are contextualized with the complex relations among Louis, Maximilian, and his son Philip of Habsburg, and Federico of Aragon. A 1503 dispatch on the newly elected Julius's professed amity towards Florence ends with a note about the prospects of France and Spain in Romagna, the former menacing Garigliano in an effort "to be masters of the sea," and the latter prudently avoiding open battle (*Leg.* November 6, 1503). In his letter to his friend, Angelo Tucci, a member of the Signoria, Machiavelli adds that both Rouen and the Pope expect the Venetians to help them in the Romagna. His reports on the political situation in Europe in May-June 1506 generate a detailed analysis of his own, disguised, as we have seen, as the reflections of others. These anonymous observers conclude that Maximilian will invade Italy, the archduke and king of England will support him while the French and Venetians oppose him, the latter's "craft" will not suffice to stop the emperor and his allies, and the emperor will be satisfied with "unopposed entry" rather than war (L. 112, June 12, 1506). Finally, in his famous *Ghiribizzi* letter to Giovan Battista Soderini, he cites a number of contemporary examples to argue his thesis that the same acts may have diverse results. Lorenzo de' Medici held on to Florence by disarming its populace, Giovanni Bentivoglio Bologna by arming them; the Vitelli in Città di Castello and the current Duke of Urbino by tearing down fortresses, Count Francesco [Sforza] of Milan and others by building them.

From the summer of 1502 to the end of 1503, a great deal of Machiavelli's attention is directed to the fiery Duke Valentino. In the context of the Arezzan revolt and the duke's expansion in the Romagna, Florence had promised him money that it hadn't paid. In his first meeting with the duke, Machiavelli was confronted with his city's alleged "bad faith." Relating this conversation, Machiavelli is sensitive to the conventions governing a strong man's efforts to command a vulnerable state's submission. The Florentines are given the rising tyrant's traditional blunt choice: you're either with me or against me. Dismissing the ambassadors' appeal to the protection of the French, he sardonically advises that they rethink their position before meeting again the next day. Implicit in this reportage is Machiavelli's impression of the duke's great strength. On June 25, they are visited by the Orsini brothers, who reinforce the duke's threats; the next morning a dispatch informs them of Vitellozzo's advances in his name. In the conclusion of his dispatch, Machiavelli admiringly comments on the duke's heroic presentation, which make him "victorious and formidable, aided by a perpetual fortune." As the encounter ends, the duke advises the Florentines to side with him, prompting Machiavelli to conjecture that he "desires to be our friend" but if not will be "our open enemy" (*Leg.* June 26, 1502).

This sense of the duke's strength of character persists even when the "conspiracy of the Magione" has made him more conciliatory toward Florence. When he reports on his first meeting with him at Imola, Machiavelli implicitly endorses his appeal even while insisting that he has related the duke's presentation in his own words. At one point he observes that the duke "appears to wish that a treaty between you and him should be made quickly" (*Leg.* October 7–8, 1502). He ends by enthusiastically conveying Valentino's request that his masters think hard on these events because if the Duke of Urbino returns from Venice, it would be to neither the Florentines' nor the duke's advantage.

Machiavelli's interpretation of the duke's attitude continues through his two-month-long stay at Imola. On the question why the duke, now employed as Florence's general, proceeds so slowly, Machiavelli conjectures that he is either delaying resigning as general or wants to see the effects of Piero Soderini's election as gonfalonier for life. In December, he comments on the infamous assassination of Ramirro d'Orca, dryly noting that "this Lord is very secretive": nobody else, not even his secretaries, knows what he's going to do since "he does not tell anything except when he orders it" (*Leg.* December 26, 1502). In his last dispatch before returning to Florence, he muses that "Duke

Valentino exhibits a fortune unheard of [and] a courage and a confidence more than human" (*Leg.* January 8, 1503).

Ironically, by this time Duke Valentino's days of glory were numbered. Still, Machiavelli had a few more occasions to record his analyses of Cesare's conduct, as well as to learn of their reception by his colleagues. In Rome in late 1503 for the election of Julius II, with the duke's fate hanging in the balance, Machiavelli begins to editorialize on his "rash confidence" in trusting in the Pope's words, then backs away, claiming that he cannot judge their intent (*Leg.* November 4, 1503). The verbal tug-of-war between Machiavelli and the duke continues. Throughout this period, the duke has been using Machiavelli to pressure Florence into aiding him in Romagna, and on November 13 he scolds them for leaving him "hanging" on their response. Machiavelli replies that though he has been giving the duke "a bit of hope" concerning the safe-conduct, the Signoria can afford to "treat him negligently" (*Leg.* November 18, 1503). The next day he reports the duke's departure for Ostia, presumably on his way to Romagna. Observing that he is "vexed" by their actions, Machiavelli warns that he may disembark at Pisa, an obvious threat to Florence, and on the day after he is indeed on his way to La Spezia, having dispatched some infantry by land towards Florence. Yet, Machiavelli adds, "everybody here laughs about his affairs" since he has had no offers of outside aid (*Leg.* November 20, 1503).

Meanwhile, the Pope has been carefully monitoring the duke's movements, and Machiavelli the Pope's. After the duke is arrested, Machiavelli, reporting a rumor that the Pope has had him thrown into the Tiber, conjectures that if it hasn't happened yet, it will, sardonically noting how this Pope pays his debts. Changing the metaphor, he adds that the duke's "sins have little by little brought him to penitence" (*Leg.* November 28, 1503). Two days later, he infers that the Pope "continues to soften" the duke by hinting that he may be released in exchange for surrendering his fortresses. Machiavelli concedes that he has difficulty foreseeing the outcome because ever since his arrival in Rome the duke's affairs have been continually deteriorating. The negotiations over the fortresses go on, the duke evidently enlisting Rouen's guarantee of the Pope's good faith, but Machiavelli is certain that the Pope is stringing them both along and that the duke is on his way out. So things stand on December 9 and 14, in the last of Machiavelli's dispatches.

Unfortunately, we have few hints as to Machiavelli's personal take on Julius II's behavior beyond registering his somewhat heartless toying with the declining Valentino. Almost all his other comments focus on the Pope's infamous entry into Perugia in September 1506. These comments virtually define Machiavelli's view of the warrior Pope. His letter to Giovan Battista Soderini, popularly known as the *Ghiribizzi* (whims, fancies), strikes the basic chord of his response to the event. The letter has broader implications for Machiavelli's worldview that will be discussed more fully later in the chapter. But one example of the fateful unpredictability of events he expounds on here is how the "disarmed" Julius—he was in fact accompanied by 150 Swiss Guard— achieved through chance what should have been difficult to achieve even "with organization and weapons" (L. 121, probably September 13–21, 1506). He gives a somewhat fuller account in his dispatch of September 13, where, as we have seen, the Pope's boldness is perfectly complemented by the docility of his reluctant host, Baglioni. In the still later version in the *Discourses*, Machiavelli contextualizes the event with the Pope's proclaimed vow to be rid of all "tyrants" who have seized land belonging to the Church. Driven by this desire, he hastens to Perugia without waiting for his troops, thus exposing himself to his enemy. Adopting his usual impersonal perspective, Machiavelli adds that "[p]rudent men who were with the Pope were astonished" by his "rashness" (*Disc.* I.27).

To begin to understand the persona implied in Machiavelli's accounts of current events, we must penetrate his pretense of detachment and diffidence. As we saw in his rebuke of the Luccan secretary, Machiavelli implicitly sees himself as his city's interpreter, a role that entails not believing everything he is told and crafting carefully what he wants others to believe. At the core of this self-conceit is the conviction that he is fulfilling his obligation to report the truth. For example, responding in 1503 to Tucci's implicit criticism of his reliability, Machiavelli points out that all the questions Tucci raises (about events in Romagna) have been answered in his "official correspondence," that is, in the *Legations*. Nevertheless, he adds ironically, "not again to fail in [his] duty" he will "reiterate" his response (L. 85, November–December 1503).[7]

Machiavelli's almost self-righteous sense that he is discharging his obligations responsibly is often couched in a rhetoric of deference.

Reporting on Valentino from Imola, he modestly leaves it to his superiors to decide what to do because they are "much more prudent and of greater experience" than he (*Leg.* October 27, 1502). A week later, he comments that he has written this "[so] that Your Lordships ... may not wonder if in the future I write to you about not getting an audience" (*Leg.* November 3, 1502). Sometimes this diffidence is grounded in a strong sense of patriotism. Uncomfortable relating the duke's offer to replace the Florentine troops in an official dispatch rather than privately, he explains that he has done so at the duke's insistence. Machiavelli is clearly uneasy about the implication that he is going beyond his brief, and so he pleads that his superiors attribute his presumption to "a natural affection that every man ought to have for his country" (*Leg.* October 16, 1502).

Occasionally, this posture is almost comically exaggerated. Machiavelli's long and precise account to Captain Ridolfi about the political situation in 1506 ends, "I know that I have bored you—forgive me; I am yours to command; and if you do not want any more of these sermons, let me know (L. 112, June 12, 1506)."[8] The letters' translators, after noting that the Italian word can mean "bibles" as well as "sermons," add that Machiavelli "chooses a politely self-effacing image" for his "lengthy disquisition."[9] Still, one can't help but sense here that Machiavelli is either hinting that he has been casting pearls before swine or else coyly inviting the Florentine commissioner general to acknowledge the profundity of his discourse. Perhaps it is up to Ridolfi to decide which implication is correct.

But beneath the occasional teasing tone in his discourse, there is a residue of genuine discontent with his position. In some circumstances, of course, apologies for his shortcomings may be warranted by the items reported, by his addressee, or by both. The last is surely the case in his account of the fall of Florence, which he ends by explaining to the unidentified lady that he has omitted "any of those matters that might offend you as being lamentable and redundant" and asks for forgiveness if he has not satisfied her (L. 203, after September 16, 1512). But beyond such special conditions, Machiavelli genuinely feels that his responsibilities surpass his social status. Of his many requests that he be relieved of this burden, two stand out, both from 1502. In June from Urbino he requests that the Signoria send him a partner because he "neither can nor wish[es to bear] such a burden alone" (*Leg.* June

26, 1502). At the very end of the year—actually, on the first day of 1503—he writes to ask that they send an ambassador, preferably someone from one of the richest and noblest families.

To put Machiavelli's view of his role and qualifications in perspective, it might be helpful to look at some letters he received from friends, acquaintances, and chancery colleagues. Many of these reflections do little more than record his correspondents' expectations of Machiavelli in doing the Republic's work.[10] Thus, Tucci writes him in Rome urging him to leak at court Florence's suspicions that the Pope is making a deal to help the Venetians gain control of Romagna (L. 82, November 21, 1503). But a number of letters to Machiavelli go on to record their authors' appreciation of that work. Often the tone of such letters becomes extreme. We have already seen his friend Vespucci's extravagant praise of his "conversation" and "spirit." Alamanno Salviati, conveying the Signoria's refusal of one of Machiavelli's requests for a discharge, goes on to reassure him that his "activities are ... of such a nature that you are the one to be begged, rather than to be begging others" (L. 67, December 23, 1502). Praising him for his Pisan victory in 1509, his friend Casavecchia goes so far as to commend him as a greater "prophet" than the Jews' (L. 169, June 17, 1509).

By far the most intimate and intriguing portrait of Machiavelli, as well as the richest texture of personal affection for him, may be gleaned from the letters of his slightly younger chancery colleague, Biaggio Buonaccorsi. Although we have no letters from Machiavelli to him, between July 1499 and August 1512 Biaggio addressed no fewer than forty-two to Machiavelli.[11] Many of these are simple pleas for Machiavelli's return from his various missions abroad and the "need here for you to take care of your business" (L. 7 and 8, July 19, 1499). Often Biaggio seasons such pleas with colorful additions. Anticipating his return from France, he obliquely alludes to a woman living near the Grazie who "is awaiting you with open figs" (L. 13, August 23, 1500). In another letter, he piquantly enjoins Machiavelli to "stick yourself in the ass" (L. 44, October 28, 1502), "Stick it up your ass" (L. 66, December 22, 1502), or simply "go scratch your ass" (L. 37, October 21, 1502). Once, he even calls him "a latrine cover" (L. 127, October 6, 1506). The bond implied by such forms of address makes it all the more puzzling that we have no trace of reciprocation by

Machiavelli. Did he find his irrepressible colleague a bore? Or, was he simply, as his friends frequently complain, too busy or blasé to reply?

Whatever the case, Biaggio's basic posture in the letters is that of a faithful, if often put-upon, friend. Writing about a mantle Machiavelli has asked him to have made for him, he twice urges him to "be patient," the second time adding, "if anything comes, I shall treat you as a friend" (L. 37, October 21, 1502). Often Biaggio seems the one who needs patience. On learning that Machiavelli has at last written a long-overdue letter to a Florentine ambassador, he assures Machiavelli that he is not angry with him. At least once, Biaggio's denial of anger with his friend opens a floodgate of complex emotions. Writing to Machiavelli at Imola about some "stories" going around, he denies being angry while cryptically alluding to various things that, if he thought about them, would quell his "affection" for him. He goes on to ostentatiously blame himself, not Machiavelli, for his own "bad choices," immediately contradicting himself by complaining of his unreciprocated love, then again reversing himself by concluding, "I wish nothing but what you wish, and enough said" (L. 35, October 15, 1502).

Despite these protestations, Biaggio clearly can be hurt by his negligent friend. The frustration of not hearing from Machiavelli is expressed in the very address of a letter to "The Most Esteemed ... Florentine Secretary ... Wherever the Hell He Is." In the body of the letter, after noting that Machiavelli has not answered his latest, Biaggio proceeds to chide him for not responding properly to communications from a Florentine ambassador to France. By this dereliction Machiavelli has brought an "admonition" upon Biaggio, which he swears will be the last such rebuke because he'll never accept a letter for Machiavelli again. You hurt yourself as much as me, he adds, before pretending to blame himself, "since I know you, and yet I keep sticking my neck out" (L. 132, October 11, 1506). Despite the almost obligatory lightening of tone that accompanies such scoldings, this letter suggests the thin line separating cajolery from real concerns about the consequences of Machiavelli's conduct.

These concerns are conveyed more directly and earnestly in Biaggio's advice to Machiavelli in a number of revealing letters on various topics. The most neutral of these regard the latter's salary. As early as his first mission to France in 1500, Biaggio reports on his successful efforts to secure an appropriation that would prevent Machiavelli's having to draw on his own resources to perform his duties. Two years later he finds himself writing to his friend at Imola that his "appropriation," along with those of two others, was denied by the Signoria. He goes on to hint that more frequent letters to the Signoria might help, figuring the latter as onions that Biaggio could present to his colleagues on his behalf. A month later, alluding again to the "actions" he has taken to see that his friend is provided for, he warns Machiavelli that his own task is made more difficult by the chancellor's murmuring that he is "a cold fish" (*cheppia*, a kind of shad) who always treated them unpleasantly (L. 65, December 21, 1502).

Perhaps the most ominous of Biaggio's warnings to Machiavelli came several years later in 1509, when he was in Mantua or Verona. Biaggio relates a bizarre story about a masked man with two witnesses who went to the house of a notary to testify that the status of Machiavelli's father Bernardo—the implication is either that he was a bastard or a debtor—disqualified his son from holding office. This incident had evidently triggered a minefield of suppressed hostility to Machiavelli. In his letter Biaggio declares that he is doing all he can to protect Machiavelli, but his adversaries "are numerous and will stop at nothing." Given these circumstances, Biaggio, as "someone who loves you [and] that you consider highly," advises him to stay where he is till the affair blows over. He closes with vague references to other citizens who second this advice (L. 181, December 28, 1509).[12]

Besides warning the absent Machiavelli, Biaggio frequently sends him invaluable reports on political activity in Florence, especially those regarding his own reputation among his colleagues. As I have already had occasion to remark, the Florentine Signoria and its several chanceries could be volatile political environments and a faithful correspondent a lifeline to the community one was serving on his missions abroad. For Machiavelli, Biaggio Buonaccorsi was an anchor in Florentine politics. As the modern translators of his letters observe, he was "the fixed point around which much of Machiavelli's active political life turned," keeping him apprised of shifts in the political landscape and looking after his reputation and private interests.[13]

Biaggio often adopts a defensive posture towards Machiavelli's enemies at home. During the tricky negotiations between Pope Julius and Duke Valentino in 1503, he reports to Machiavelli in Rome that Florentine public opinion favors the Pope, adding in code that, unlike

Machiavelli himself, most of the citizens oppose lending the duke aid and feel that it's the Pope who holds the upper hand. Worse, he adds, some of his fellow citizens accuse Machiavelli of seeking "some indemnity" (L. 76, November 15, 1503). A few weeks later, Biaggio again reports trouble, this time coming from Agnolo Tucci. Angry that Machiavelli hasn't brought him up to date on matters in France and Romagna, Tucci is said to be bad-mouthing Machiavelli around town with some success. Even while warning Machiavelli against such malice, Biaggio assures his friend that he has done his best to counter this gossip. On the other hand he asserts that those who are advising Machiavelli to find another position don't love him as he does.

Despite Biaggio's mercurial temperament—his racy language, his extravagant professions of love—the dominant impression his letters to Machiavelli convey is of an older brother (though he is in fact younger) trying his best to contain his overeager sibling. At one point Biaggio warns of the limited efficacy of fine rhetoric. Another time he reports that the infrequency of Machiavelli's dispatches from the allied camp has aroused real animosity in the commissioner of Cascina, one Niccolò Capponi. Biaggio hints that Machiavelli's popularity with the militia, coupled with his irresponsibility as a correspondent, has provoked Capponi to lodge a formal complaint with the Ten about not receiving enough information from him.[14] The following day Biaggio prescribes patience since powerful men always merit our respect. Therefore, he urges Machiavelli to placate Capponi with some letters, adding that Piero Soderini himself seconds his advice. This double-barreled plea for patience underscores Machiavelli's correspondents' uneasiness about his temperament. Suppressed anxiety on this score is implied by the salutation of a letter to Machiavelli in Rome, which Biaggio signs (in Latin) "As a brother" (L. 72, November 2, 1503).

If Biaggio's often exuberant letters to Machiavelli give us a unique insight into the private nature of this supremely public man, the latter does not always come across as the cautious, self-effacing servant of his country he strives so hard to appear. We will see later on how a number of his letters—the famous account of his routine in retirement, the ribald fictionalization of his friends' sexual exploits of both kinds and of his own encounter with an old whore, the description of the prank deployed against the unsuspecting friars at Carpi, and others—reveal the spirit, humor, and occasionally darker side of the man. But to stick for the moment to his conception of his public role, we might end by considering the famous *Ghiribizzi*, his letter to Giovan Battista Soderini, the gonfalonier's nephew, written at Perugia sometime in September 1506.

Though one of Machiavelli's best-known letters, its occasion is shrouded in mystery. Not only is its precise date in dispute—most editors say between September 13 and 21, but Giorgio Inglese for one would extend this to September 27—but it is hard to see what in the brief letter of Giovan Battista's it is responding to, or for that matter what in his relations with Machiavelli in general could have provoked such a response.[15] A possible solution to this mystery lies in a throwaway line in Giovan Battista's letter. After announcing amiably that he has nothing to say to Machiavelli, he excuses his writing anyway by alluding to his "practice of doing innumerable things aimlessly" (L. 119, September 12, 1506). This note of whimsical serendipity may well have struck a responsive chord in its reader upon rereading it, as he says he did. At this point, Machiavelli evidently inscribed one of the six marginalia that reflect on his text: "He who does not know how to fence can entangle one who does." At first blush, the comment is in the writer's usual self-deprecating mode. By rereading, and implicitly, rewriting Soderini's letter, the artless recipient may entrap his skilled adversary. But as the letter unfolds, the marginalia work against its author. It is Machiavelli who will trip himself up in the rambling reflections that follow (L. 121, September 13–21, 1506).

This self-dialogue, self-interrogation, and ultimately self-contradiction pervades Machiavelli's famous reflections on the letter's apparent thesis that the same acts can lead to different, and different acts to the same, outcomes. Framing his historical reflections is the paradox that men's actions and their results seem to fall into no discernible pattern. As the letter concludes, wise men should always understand and thus adapt to the times. Unfortunately, "such wise men do not exist: ... thus it follows that Fortune is fickle, controlling men and keeping them under her yoke." This being the case, the Machiavellian impulse to make sense of human events is doomed to be thwarted. As readers of Chapter 25 of *The Prince* will recall—and as I will detail later—fortune's whimsies will trump the best of our efforts to rationalize our existence. Even her most stalwart adversary will prevail only half the time. How, in short, is the mental agility Machiavelli so prides himself on to cope with the irrationality of events?

The answer to this question is implicit in his marginalia, of which the first serves as a capstone. By stepping outside of his own intellectual struggle with the inchoateness of events, Machiavelli can enact the competition of ignorant entangler and knowledgeable fencer, thus providing a model of consciousness more in tune with the variability of things. This model is implied by the letter's meditation on its own proceedings. Reflecting on the paradox that his rereading of Soderini's letter led him to ignore the latter's injunction not to answer it, he explains that he would be surprised at this reaction were it not that he is rarely surprised by men's deeds. In other words, well before he introduces the problem of the mismatch between human acts and their consequences, Machiavelli constructs himself as someone whose mind is capable of transcending the normal demand for rational consistency. This is further underscored by his claim to have "savored" the affairs of men.[16] If, as we've seen, the allegedly nonexistent wise man is one who can match his acts to the perverse fluctuations of fortune, the letter implicitly nominates its author as the living exception to its own argument, the clumsy entangler of its alter ego's adroit fencing.

The internal dialogue is projected onto the external one with Soderini. Turning from his own motives to those of his interlocutor, Machiavelli somewhat equivocally asserts his appreciation of the latter's "prudence." But the discursive path to this climactic compliment is so twisted as to virtually negate its own affirmation. To begin with, its assertion is literally parenthetical. And even within the parenthesis, it is equivocally lodged in a "perspective" that is contrasted with that of "the many": whereas Soderini's perspective considers "nothing but prudence," Machiavelli's must take into account "the ends, not the means, of things." It is at best a tossup which perspective is superior, but in any case the writer clearly disassociates himself from his addressee.

This tension is enhanced by the metaphor that governs the buildup to Machiavelli's praise of Soderini's "prudence." In complimenting his young friend, he refers to the "compass" of his "navigation." But in context the figure is less definitively complimentary. The main predication of the sentence asserts the writer's own act of comprehension: "I know you" and your "compass." The sentence then immediately injects a potential note of criticism of that compass: "even if it could be blamed, which it cannot be, I should not, since I see what ports it has guided you to." In the original version of the sentence Machiavelli had written, "what status it had honored you with." But the substitution strengthens the nautical metaphor while hinting at the young man's "duplicity."[17] Hence, the latter's "compass" is implicitly qualified by Machiavelli's moral knowledge of his man, much as his own response had been by his intuitions of the ways of "men." By the time we reach the parenthetical praise of Soderini's "prudence," the perspective in which it alone is visible has been co-opted by that of the writer with its inherently superior grasp of reality.

The *Ghiribizzi*, then, arguably epitomizes the Secretary's real view of his own place in the grander scheme of things. Putting into perspective his many expressions of diffidence regarding his role, it seems to bear out the flattering views of his friends and colleagues during the period of his active political life. Even before the public debut of Machiavelli the writer, there are signs in his private letters of the complex and playful imagination of an astute observer of the human scene. We will see that imagination at work in his correspondence when we return to the subject of the "literary" Machiavelli in Chapter 6. But it is important to note at the outset that implicit in his self-conception even during his preliterary phase is his consciousness of the impossibility of human wisdom.

CHAPTER 3

MACHIAVELLI AS POLITICAL PHILOSOPHER

To most of us Machiavelli is less a model of civic engagement than a political thinker. Indeed, in at least one standard understanding of Machiavelli, he is the ur-political theorist, the arch-defender of tyrants. For those imbued with this bias, it may be useful to briefly survey the texts in which Machiavelli most clearly states his political philosophy. These are his most scandalous work, *The Prince*; his most sustained practical analysis of republican politics, the *Discourses on the First Ten Books of Titus Livy* (or just *Discourses*); and, though it is primarily a historical work, the *Florentine Histories*.

The Prince is the first written of the three. Composed shortly after his fall from grace early in 1513, it was explicitly designed to win the arch-republican Machiavelli employment with the newly restored Medici princes.[1] The circumstances of its writing raise questions about its tone. In dedicating what was to become his masterpiece first to Lorenzo the Magnificent's son, Giuliano, Duke of Nemours (who died soon after its completion), then to Lorenzo's grandson (and Giuliano's nephew), Lorenzo, Duke of Urbino, Machiavelli seemed to endorse its explicit packaging as a how-to manual for tyrants. Quickly narrowing his focus first to principalities, then to those that have been newly acquired, he outlines the skills demanded of those who would govern such acquisitions, including a "city accustomed to freedom," that is, a republic (Chapter 5).[2] In its closing chapter (Chapter 26), Machiavelli steps out of the text's framework to exhort an unnamed Redeemer who will unite Italy and liberate her from "barbarian occupation." All of these parameters, as well as the details of its argument, reflect the circumstances of its composition in the months, possibly even weeks, following the demise of the Republic.[3]

The *Discourses'* dates of composition are more problematic. Having taken notes on Livy's history of Rome, at some point Machiavelli decided to expand on them in a series of discourses that would constitute a general treatise on republics. This work-in-progress is almost certainly what he refers to when he says in Chapter 2 of *The Prince* that he has "spoken at length elsewhere" about republics. But if it's clear enough that the *Discourses* were under way by the time Machiavelli began writing *The Prince*, it's much less certain when they were completed. It is possible that they were never in any real sense "completed" at all, but only temporarily suspended in 1513 to write *The Prince*, then again in 1519 to take up *The Art of War*. In any event, by the time he moved back to Florence from his country estate in February 1514, he had in his possession part of the *Discourses* as well as a manuscript of *The Prince*.[4]

With the *Histories* we are once again on surer footing. Less ambiguously than *The Prince*, this text is a product of Machiavelli's relationship with the Medici. After writing the *Art of War* in 1519 and finishing the *Life of Castruccio Castracani* in 1520, he was engaged by Cardinal Giulio de' Medici to write a history of his native city, receiving his official commission from the University in November of the latter year. By the time he had finished the first eight books, the Cardinal had become Pope Clement VII, and Machiavelli presented the revised manuscript to the new Pope in 1525. From the outset, he was unsure at what date to begin his account. His first plan was to start the narrative in 1434, with the return from exile of Cosimo the Elder; then he added an initial book going back to the city's origins. Likewise, he may have initially intended to bring it down to his own time. But at the time of Cardinal Giulio's accession in 1523, he had finished his account in Book Eight of the new Pope's uncle, Lorenzo, who died in 1492, and there he decided to leave it. After revising the manuscript, he employed his friend Vettori in Rome to help negotiate its presentation, went there to present it at the end of May 1525, and was rewarded in June with a gift of 120 gold ducats.

The Prince presents formidable challenges to anyone seeking clues there to Machiavelli's political philosophy. One way is to read it as an ironic "book of Republicans," as did Rousseau, who noted in the *Social*

Contract that "[w]hile appearing to instruct kings, he has done much to educate the people."[5] The problem with this tack is that it is based on circular reasoning. If we assume that because of his background and his other writings Machiavelli can't possibly mean what he says about princes and power in *The Prince*, we easily arrive at the conclusion that everything he states there is written with tongue in cheek. There are similar problems with taking the text "straight." This is Leo Strauss's mistake in *Thoughts on Machiavelli*, which he begins with the unqualified declaration that Machiavelli was a "teacher of evil."[6] Since the author clearly expects the potential rulers he addresses to apply his maxims on acquiring and maintaining power, the argument goes, he must personally espouse even the most extreme measures the text recommends. Here the problem is a failure of historical contextualization. To take the book's precepts straight is to ignore the fact that its author *was* a republican addressing powerful potential patrons who have indeed recently acquired states.

There is, of course, some truth in both of these views. In writing *The Prince*, Machiavelli does seem to be belying both his own experience in governing and his deeply held republican principles. It is therefore virtually impossible that he "means" what the book says in the sense that he wants his own city to be ruled according to its precepts. In fact, we know that he did not. Hence what he "teaches" in *The Prince* must be in some sense ironic. By the same token, Machiavelli's anatomy of authoritarian rule is "true"—that is, his experience of politics is too important for him to set down axioms of governance he does not believe to be correct. He had read deeply in history and was an astute observer of contemporary political life. In writing about how successful princes conduct themselves, he stakes his credibility on the accuracy of his observations, especially in a work designed to win him gainful employment.

This is the premise governing Machiavelli's self-presentation in the text. Though his dedicatory address ends on a note of abject self-pity by one suffering the "malignity of fortune," it begins by vaunting the petitioner's "knowledge of the actions of great men," acquired through both experience and reading. This claim is reinforced at the center of the work, where Machiavelli again asserts his *bona fides* as a truth-teller (Chapter 15). Announcing his intention to truly be of use to his reader, he rejects time-worn ideals of governance in favor of "the effectual truth of the matter." Though one should never underestimate Machiavelli's cunning in textually refashioning himself, I believe this is a helpful clue as to how *The Prince* should be read. The famous phrase translated above, *la verità effettuale della cosa*, constitutes the text's central claim. While it is difficult to capture the precise connotation of Machiavelli's *effettuale*, its derivation from *effetto* (effect) points to actual events in the everyday world. Neither an ironic exposé nor a naive endorsement of autocratic principalities, the text is a truthful record of its author's hard-won understanding of them, set forth in a vein of tough-minded realism. As we shall see, this intention is the cornerstone of the work's political philosophy.

No one familiar with Machiavelli's biography will be surprised to find that military affairs lie at the heart of that philosophy. For this reason those chapters that deal with military matters, Chapters 12–14 and 20, are central to both the argument and the organization of the work. Machiavelli spells out this relationship at the beginning of the first of these chapters. The previous eleven have detailed the "natures of . . . states," why they wax or wane, and how they are acquired and lost. Now he must discuss the acts that win or lose them. Reiterating that a prince must establish "strong foundations" if he is to survive, he identifies these foundations as "good laws and good arms." For Machiavelli the two goods are virtually identical. As he goes on to say, "there cannot be good laws where there are not good arms, and where there are good arms there are bound to be good laws" (Chapter 12).

This almost formulaic equation of laws and arms is complicated in Chapter 20, on building fortresses and related issues. Here the immediately preceding and succeeding chapters concern reputation. Introduced at the end of Chapter 15 by the distinction between an apparent virtue that may bring ruin and an apparent vice that may bring security, this key segment of *The Prince* discusses the relative efficacy of liberality and stinginess (Chapter 16) and of cruelty and clemency (Chapter 17). These topics are elaborated in Chapter 19 with multiple examples of how new princes have conducted themselves in general. Here building fortresses is treated under the rubric of holding on to newly acquired territories. In this framework fortresses are viewed as potentially useful for those fearing their own subjects, but can be ignored by those fearing foreigners more. The best fortress is to not be hated by your own populace. Hence, building fortresses may be good or bad, depending on the circumstances; but that prince is a fool who, trusting in fortresses, "thinks he need not worry about the enmity of his people."

The centrality of reputation in Chapter 20 underscores the conception of power politics set forth in these important chapters. To a degree almost Shakespearean, Machiavelli brilliantly grasps the essential theatricality of political action. At the heart of his political philosophy is the understanding that politicians are players, actors upon a public stage who must seduce the minds of their audience. For him, "reputation" signifies "public image," is almost always positive, and is closely allied semantically with "virtue" and "prudence."[7] This fundamental axiom explains the platitudes in Chapter 19 on avoiding contempt and hatred. But it also governs the important discussion in Chapter 18, somewhat misleadingly advertised as dealing with how princes should keep their word. This discussion begins on-theme by condoning everyone's privileging "integrity" over "craftiness." Yet before the opening sentence is over, Machiavelli acknowledges the superior success of one who can "manipulate the minds of men craftily." This preference for "astuteness," with its secondary connotation of deceptiveness, controls the chapter's—and indeed the book's—central teaching. To be a successful ruler, one must know how to govern men's minds. To do so is to secure one's "reputation."

What is most surprising here is what happens to the idea of control as Machiavelli works out his conception of political action. Having stated at the outset that his topic is manipulating men's minds by craft, he proceeds to the famous distinction between the human method of fighting with laws and the bestial one of fighting with force. Having resolved the distinction via the figure of Chiron, half man half beast, he substitutes another dichotomy: craft and force, the fox and the lion. Here again one must opt for both: the lion to deal with wolves, the fox with traps. We would all prefer, he concedes, to act solely like the noble lion. But because men are "a sad lot," in order to flourish you too must act in bad faith, must indeed be "a great liar and hypocrite." With what one feels is great personal relish, Machiavelli invokes the example of Pope Alexander VI, who was always successful and never hesitated to deceive.

At this juncture Machiavelli hits his stride. Stepping back from his instruction, he reflects that in politics it is not *having* great virtues but *seeming* to have them that counts. More, if you have them and exercise them they hurt you, whereas if you only *seem* to have them they can be "useful." It is good to appear truthful, and so forth, and it is also good to be so. But in a pinch you must be prepared to sacrifice the reality to the appearance. And this capacity, while it is justified by the need to preserve the state, centers on the ruler's state of mind. In striving to maintain power order in the state, the prince "must keep [his] mind ... disposed" to duplicity, "ready to shift as the winds of fortune ... may dictate." Here, for the first time in our discussion, we meet a central Machiavellian trope. As we will see in Chapter 5, problematic as it is for the rugged individualist who seeks to master his world, to yield oneself to fortune is a posture to which Machiavelli repeatedly reverts.

Here we reach the paradox at the heart of Machiavelli's political anthropology. Throughout the discussion leading up to it he argues for controlling external circumstances by keeping a realistic grasp of human affairs. Having a firm grip on the differences between being and seeming, the latter is free to be lion or fox: to be as he seems or not as conditions demand. It is a matter of choice, and the good ruler will not hesitate to resort to duplicity if need be. But here, at the existential center of the discussion, Machiavelli seems to stumble on a very different conceit. Far from being outside of and apart from the world he must control, the prince's mind partakes of its essence. It must be prepared, when circumstances dictate, to become part of the very chaos of things.

Machiavelli backs away from this scandal even before the chapter concludes. After all, in his own mind he is not a philosopher but a practical man of action—or, if this is no longer in the cards, an adviser to such men. Hence he quickly returns to his theme of "reputation," extrapolating from the interior world of mind to the external one of appearances. The audience of the ruler's deceptions is "the masses," who are governed by appearances and results. Therefore the prince should always act with an eye to how his conduct impresses the many. This premise continues to govern Chapter 19, where he concludes that a prince's chief concern is "to satisfy the populace by making them happy." With this conclusion, Machiavelli has come back to political *terra firma*. The end of governing is to preserve order, and what does *that* also makes people happy. Though the threat of internal disorder may occasionally rear its ugly head in Machiavellian discourse, the reassuring thought of the simplicity of the masses brings him back to the bedrock of his political philosophy—the securing of human happiness and thus of order in the state.

Implicit in the discussion so far is a vindication of "Machiavellism."[8] Much discussion of the work has focused on its alleged thesis that the end of government justifies its means. This emphasis, I would argue, runs the risk of obscuring the text's primary concern with good government, which aims at maintaining a rational order in the state and thus securing the general happiness of the governed. More central to Machiavelli's project in *The Prince*, however, is its implied hierarchy of ends. One such end is reputation, in the Machiavellian scheme of things an instrument for securing power. Power in turn must be wielded to impose order, and order is required to guarantee human happiness. The terminus in this causal chain is not power, but happiness. Nevertheless, Machiavelli is a realist, and realistically each link in the chain is the means to an end, which implicitly *does* justify it. Reputation is necessary for power, power for order, and order for happiness. Moreover, the initial link in the chain may be duplicity. While the *reputation* for honesty may be a prerequisite for achieving power, order, and happiness, the reality is not required and may even on occasion be a hindrance. For Machiavelli, in short, political institutions lead to an ironic "denaturalization of man" in the constant struggle to redeem human nature from corruption.[9] Such is the scandalous conclusion of a man who prefers plain speaking to "what people have imagined."

Being concerned, at least nominally, with the Roman Republic, the *Discourses* come much closer than *The Prince* to depicting Machiavelli's republican ideal.[10] This conclusion is strongly implied in the work's dedication, in which the author claims to have "set down all that I know ... about ... political affairs." Under the guise of providing a book-by-book commentary on Livy's history of Rome, the *Discourses* cover a wide range of topics, from the best form of government, to the pros and cons of dictatorship, to the proper role of the populace, to expansion, diplomacy, war, and conspiracies to preserving freedom. These topics are gathered in three books loosely organized around the development of Rome's constitution, the growth of its empire, and the example of its great men. Let me extrapolate and arrange in a more-or-less logical order the chief components of the text's implied political philosophy.

As always with Machiavelli, understanding political institutions begins with grasping the nature of men. The latter inevitably centers on what he calls *virtù*, an untranslatable Italian term descended from the Latin *virtus* (from *vir*, man), whose meanings range from strength of character, to generic "excellence," to essential function (the virtue of a knife is to cut), to modern ethical "virtue." In some of his most memorable texts, Machiavelli pairs this keyword with its opposite number, "fortune," to construct an existential drama between self and other. I will return to these keywords in the next two chapters. But for now it may be helpful to view Machiavelli's anthropology outside the narrow frame of *virtù/fortuna* and consider how its main components underpin his theory of government.

Machiavelli's fundamental view of men is anything but sunny. His narrative of the founding of Rome's most characteristic institutions quickly underscores their rootedness in unruly human nature. That nature is unvarying—men "have, and always have had, the same passions" (*Disc.* III.43)—and a firm grasp of this premise underlies all political achievements. An example is the appointment of tribunes of the plebs to check the power of the Senate. In creating this office, Roman legislators rightly assumed "that all men are wicked" and will seize any occasion to express their wickedness. Having treated the plebs well until the Tarquins were expelled, the Senate then started oppressing them, showing that men rarely do good unless they have to. A few chapters later, Machiavelli justifies public trials before judges because they furnish an outlet for men's "malignant humours" (*Disc.* I.7). Here we meet the peculiarly Machiavellian use of *umori* to denote the innately evil predilections of human beings. Nothing in his vast oeuvre contradicts Machiavelli's basically gloomy view of humanity.

Paradoxically, this grimly conceived human nature underwrites the best of human endeavors. Machiavelli sees political life as the collective harnessing of the most destructive elements in men's individual makeup. At the opening of Book Two, he spells out at great length the three fundamental axioms on which the great founders constructed their empires. First, "human affairs are [always in] flux." This is the basic condition each of us faces in seeking to order our lives; but, for Machiavelli imposing such order is possible only collectively through political acts, the most primitive of which is to constitute a state. Secondly, the world has always contained "as much good as ... evil."

However shaky the human foundations on which states are erected, it is always possible that they can maximize the good and contain the evil. Finally, because "human appetites are insatiable ... the human mind is perpetually discontented." This assertion generates the challenge that lies at the heart of all human endeavors. While we can suppress our baser natures through collective action, to make that effort requires that we overcome the self-knowledge that prompts us to deny the very possibility of success. Though our highest aspirations can never be satisfied, we must focus on the preponderance of good manifested in all human achievements.

Machiavelli's paradoxically upbeat take on collective human efforts is visible everywhere in the *Discourses*. In praising the founders and condemning the destroyers of religions or states, he concludes that all men will want to emulate the good, contrasting Tarquin with good rulers who blessed their subjects with "security and contentment" (*Disc.* III.5). The Roman conquerors' "liberality" arises from the souls of preeminent individuals but redounds to the glory of their states, transcending the individuals' rank or station. Hence a great general can call forth the best qualities in his men by urging them to emulate his courage in battle. In sum, Machiavelli's faith that the good in men outshines their evil extends from the battlefield to the forum, from allies to adversaries, and from military leaders to their men.

Every facet of Machiavelli's anthropology contributes to his theory of government. Most of its tenets spring from his conception of a universal human desire for liberty. Almost any development in a free city will "promote the cause of freedom" (*Disc.* I.29). Further enhancing that freedom is the willingness of citizens to subordinate personal offenses to love of country. Nevertheless, maintaining freedom is difficult, especially if a city has been living under a corrupted prince. Even good institutions are not good in a "corrupted state," where power-seekers prevent men of excellence from ruling (*Disc.* I.18). As restoring political life requires a good man and resorting to violence a bad one, it's impossible either to preserve or to create a republican form of government in corrupt states. Such is the precarious balance between the necessity of liberty and the perils that attend it.

Despite the numerous examples of virtuous individuals, in Machiavelli's view the burden of maintaining freedom must be borne by the many. This assumption is at the heart of his democratic republicanism.

Although his understanding of *virtù* tends to locate greatness of spirit in "great" men, he by no means denies it to ordinary people, especially when they are united in solidarity. Machiavelli doesn't hesitate to privilege the populace over a prince. Cicero and others are simply wrong, he says, in holding that the masses tend to be "variable, fickle and ungrateful" when in power. While both people and princes are inconstant when not constrained by laws, princes are more so. And since the populace is more prudent, stable, and wise than princes, rule by the former is better than by the latter. Elsewhere, he maintains that "The Plebs United is Strong, [though] in Itself it is Weak" (*Disc.* I.57) and concludes that the populace has fewer flaws than the prince and is therefore more trustworthy. Such pronouncements clearly imply that for Machiavelli freedom in a state rests on the strength of its people.

Despite the fact that the achievements of collectivities outstrip those of individuals, some aspects of human nature require governance. Though he is not unduly pessimistic about his fellow creatures, Machiavelli readily acknowledges that in human activities some evil is always "bound up with what is good" (*Disc.* III.37). Even in groups men are easily corrupted; hence it is necessary for legislators to punish their misconduct, especially when it masquerades as benevolence. As one chapter title puts it, "The Populace, misled by the False Appearance of Advantage, often seeks its own Ruin, and is easily moved by Splendid Hopes and Rash Promises" (*Disc.* I.53). Perhaps the greatest of these potentially ruinous appetites is ambition, which inevitably generates enmity and, eventually, disaster. On the other hand, the *absence* of ambition would deny the expansiveness required to maintain a free republic. This need to expand is another troublesome element of human nature that requires governance. Machiavelli concedes that a non-expansive, stable republic like Sparta or Venice can achieve peace and harmony. But even so, human nature seems to compel expansion, as the Roman model attests.

Overarching all these constraints is the need to submit to something greater than the self. Most readers tend to be skeptical whenever Machiavelli speaks of the role of religion in human affairs, and there is no denying that his pronouncements often seem to be merely instrumental, as when he claims that religion helps bind men by oaths, miracles keep people obedient, or rulers need to uphold religion even if they are convinced that it's specious. Conversely, he observes that the Roman Catholic Church's loss of all religious devotion has kept Italy divided. Lest we infer from these examples that Machiavelli's religion is so instrumental as to preclude a god, we may note that he finds the "fear of God" Numa gave his fellow Romans conducive to obedience; even Florence, he adds, was "persuaded" by Savonarola (*Disc.* I.11).[11] Is the author of these sentiments the penitent who is said to have called for the last rites of the Church on his deathbed? Perhaps. But Machiavelli can't leave the subject without commenting that when the pious Samnites resorted to religion to reverse their string of defeats by the Romans, they were easily overcome by the latter's superior *virtù* (*Disc.* I.15).[12]

Discussing how human nature sustains collective governance raises the question of just what good government *is*. To begin with, for Machiavelli it is mixed government.[13] Rehearsing the three good and three bad forms of government in the opening discourses of Book One, he argues that Principality, Aristocracy, and Democracy respectively morph into Tyranny, Oligarchy, and Anarchy. None of these mutations is satisfactory, the bad ones because of their inherent evil, the good because they're short-lived. For that reason, primitive lawgivers wisely opted for a mixed state, in Rome first a blend of monarchy and oligarchy and then of both with democracy. The establishment of tribunes as the key to Roman freedom is axiomatic for Machiavelli. In his view it's the populace rather than the aristocracy that safeguards liberty, since trouble normally comes from the haves, who are uneasy about what they've got.

The people are also the key to mixed government's success, mainly because of their numerical superiority. There are simply more who seek freedom from oppression than there are who desire to oppress. Since he privileges the well-being of the community over that of individuals, Machiavelli urges a republic to imitate Rome and use "everybody in the city," thus ensuring an abundance of virtuous men (*Disc.* I.30). It is better, he adds, to have the public as a whole for friends and men of influence for enemies than the reverse. Another important corollary is that, like the early Romans, citizens should be content with poverty, which endues the city with "honour," leaving "profits" to the public (*Disc.* I.25).

Such privileging of communal over individual interests generates several specific strictures. One is that all measures must be undertaken to save the life and preserve the freedom of one's country. Another is the importance of allocating rewards and punishments, since in a republic "Severity" may prove more effective than "Sociability" in securing the public good (*Disc.* III.22). Conversely, no citizen should expect to do wrong with impunity, since the resulting insolence would soon annihilate civic life. A final imperative is goodwill on the part of rulers. Reversing Chapters 17 and 19 of *The Prince*, in the *Discourses* Machiavelli holds that it is better to be loved than feared. This is strongly implied in the examples of "humanity" in *Discourse* III.20, from which he infers that a gentle act can be more efficacious than a harsh one. Though he concedes in the next discourse that either fear or kindness can work if one has *virtù*, his basic conviction seems to be that, other things being equal, one should temper one's severity towards one's "subjects" and treat one's "associates" humanely. In general, nothing is gained by "making [one]self odious" (*Disc.* III.19).

A major component of good government for Machiavelli is territorial expansiveness. Since expansiveness is innate in men, the question of how a *state* should expand becomes crucial. Of the three possibilities he recognizes, Machiavelli holds subjecting other states, as the Spartans and Athenians did, to be the worst because such states have no allies to assist them and enhance their population. Conversely, the best method is the Roman way of forming alliances, as allies will unthinkingly fall under your yoke; next best are leagues based on equality like the Tuscans and the Swiss. Above all, successful expansion must be voluntary. Those men obeying the orders of rulers, most notably mercenaries, will never match the virtue of those fighting for themselves. Though men's *virtù* may be a constant, their attitude toward their rulers will be different and their courage will vary according to whether they fight freely or for pay. Finally, if expansiveness is indeed a universal human trait, it is most productive in a self-governing polity where everybody shares the spiritual, as well as the material, spoils.

A few tenets bear a uniquely Machiavellian charge. Fundamental among them is the moral superiority of republics. Though like any form of state they are not immortal, republics live longer and more fully than principalities. Subscribing to a modified theory of inertia in human affairs, Machiavelli believes that once one line of conduct works, men are reluctant to try another. Hence republican institutions are slow to change, since everybody in a republic must embrace the proposed change to give it traction. This is especially true regarding the willful surrender of liberty, a topic on which Machiavelli can at times sound fairly pessimistic. As one chapter title has it, "If those City-States which from the Outset have been Free, as Rome was, find it difficult to formulate Laws whereby to maintain Liberty, those which have just been servile are faced with a Quasi-impossibility" (*Disc.* I.49).

Republics are resilient. Machiavelli boldly asserts that "a bad citizen cannot do much harm in a republic that is not corrupt" (*Disc.* III.8). This notion is developed in the longest of Machiavelli's discourses, III.6, where he argues that conspiracies against one's country can only occur when a republic is corrupt. In general, few conspiracies are successful, and again those directed against one's country can only succeed in a corrupt republic. From this fact he infers that those who would overthrow a government must proceed differently in a corrupt city than in one not corrupt. One who would impose a "bad form" on a republic must first find a "disordered . . . material," usually one disordered over several generations (*Disc.* III.8). The odds against overthrowing a virtuous republic are distinctly unfavorable. Nevertheless, contrary to most political thinkers, Machiavelli consistently identifies discord as a potential source of political progress, as in the prolonged struggle between the Roman Senate and plebs. As their experience bears out, the aspirations of a free people rarely threaten freedom itself.

Good government entails several other conditions peculiar to Machiavelli. Consider his advice on how to unite a previously divided city. The worst course of action is to force the warring parties to make peace, the best to kill the opposing leaders; but given the general debility of his contemporaries, the most acceptable is to banish or imprison them. Once a city has been unified, keeping it so is a great challenge. Here, like several of our own founding fathers, Machiavelli subscribes to the principle of periodic revival. Like all finite entities, a state must regularly be renewed if it is to survive, as was Rome while it was still uncorrupted.[14] One of Machiavelli's prescriptions for maintaining a well-functioning state seems to spring directly from his secretarial experience. As he learned early, giving advice in a manner that encourages its acceptance is difficult. Hence in public discourse, whether addressing a republic or a prince, a citizen should give advice sparingly and defend his own views humbly. That way, even if ignored, one will profit, at least in one's own self-esteem. In any case, keeping silent is not an option.

In Machiavelli's view, with the right props a well-constituted republic can sustain itself indefinitely. To do so, however, requires strong men. Being unprepared to fight, the weak are potential pawns in the hands of the great forces governing human events. Conversely, taking up arms inoculates a state against the whims of fortune. Nor does he ignore the role of religion. Not only does he credit Roman religion with making the tribunes obey the consuls and the consuls spare the plebs the agony of war, but he even implies that it fostered peace, order, and the acquisition of territory. On the other hand, the Samnites were propelled into battle against the Romans by the oath imposed by their priests. But in the last resort it is the rulers who are responsible for keeping the state strong. The military unpreparedness of contemporary princes and republics shames their leaders: "if where there are men, there are not soldiers, it is their ruler's fault" (*Disc.* I.21).

Up to now our discussion of Machiavelli's political theory has been fairly positive. There are, however, some aspects of establishing and maintaining a state that raise red flags, even for Machiavelli. A few of these are simply elements intrinsic to government that must be overcome if order and stability are to be achieved. Others are sometimes unpleasant imperatives in the conduct of collective human affairs. Though lumping them together in a single discussion runs the risk of conveying a somewhat dismal view of the possibility of successful governance, in context these qualifications tend to confirm our general impression that on balance Machiavelli is a realist.

The greatest challenges to successful governing may be conveniently grouped under the single rubric "corruption." Invoking the paradigm of form and matter to explain human affairs, Machiavelli instinctively assumes that if the basic human material in a state is corrupt, no form imposed on it can be viable. Conversely, if a republic is *not* corrupt, it can withstand many dangers. For this reason, conspiracies will succeed only in a corrupt republic, while power bestowed for too long a time, even if freely conferred by the populace, can be harmful. Among the many forms of corruption Machiavelli acknowledges, perhaps the one insuperable one is the presence of those who perform no useful work and live idly off their estates. Though only slightly worse than those who lord it over others from their castles, these "gentry" constitute an equally insuperable obstacle to the equality necessary for a healthy republic.

Equally pernicious are the inclination to vilify others and the difficulty of submitting to the state. Lacking restraint, calumnies provoke discord and can even bring down republics, and Machiavelli insists that calumniators should be severely punished. The problem of submission in a republic is knottier, being rooted in the human desire for freedom. Still, Machiavelli ironically sees it as less of a challenge to moderns than to the ancients, since submission to a collective is easier for contemporary Italians than, say, for the Samnites, who defended liberty ferociously. Freedom is less valued today because Christianity denigrates worldly reputation. The violence of ancient sacrifices contrasts starkly with Christianity's teaching men patient resignation to affronts.

To overcome these endemic obstacles to good government, Machiavelli offers a number of do's and don'ts. Of these the most characteristically "Machiavellian" is the occasional need to do evil. Usually associated in *The Prince* with the acquisition of new states, this imperative generates some of the most memorable passages in his writings. The *Discourses* likewise acknowledge that good may come of evil. Rooted in the drive to expand, social evil begins with the injunction to cleanse the scene of its corruption. Whether a principality or a republic, a new state *must* secure itself to endure. This imperative is especially applicable to people accustomed to living under a prince. Though the *virtù* necessary to preserve their liberty has been dormant, they must learn to spare no one who conspires against the new regime. In maintaining order, however, certain measures are to be avoided. A ruler or rulers should at all costs avoid breaking a newly promulgated law or inflicting injuries needlessly. If killing those resisting the new order is necessary, it should be done quickly. In addition, one should take pains not to humiliate one's enemies lest one arouse their ire.

Not surprisingly, war occupies a special place in Machiavelli's political theory. Several specific attributes define the role of military virtue in a strong republic. One is that old warhorse, reputation. Anyone attacking an army thought to have been weakened by a previous battle will be deceived because the reputation gained by victory more than compensates for the loss of men in battle. Equally commendable in war is the use of fraud, especially when outfoxing the enemy. It is also important to exercise discretion in judging a subject people. Whereas the Romans rightly either pardoned or annihilated the conquered Latins, the Florentines foolishly banished some Arezzans but let their city stand. Finally, honor and virtue aside, war being by nature an exercise in excess, Machiavelli has nothing but scorn for those who would confine its practitioners within a narrow set of rules. Roman generals, he notes approvingly, were never severely punished for their errors, even if they brought injury to the Republic, because if they had been none would have ever tried to excel.

The *Florentine Histories* constitute a mostly negative case study in governing. As the circumstances of its composition suggest, Machiavelli's concern here is to anatomize the countless events that brought his own city, and Italy, to their present pass. Not unexpectedly, war and military excellence play an outsized role in his assessment of this history. But if for Machiavelli war demands the utmost exercise of human ability, it is those qualities that inform the larger story of a nation. Machiavelli's narrative in the *Histories* abundantly illustrates his countrymen's historic struggle to overcome the evil inherent in men and create the highest possible "order," a republic.[15]

At his most fatalistic, Machiavelli posits an iron progression in human affairs, in which order generates virtue, virtue quiet, quiet leisure, leisure disorder, and disorder ruin. If this cycle is ultimately supervised by a distant God, Who sends disasters to remind men of His power, its true presiding deity is Fortuna, as I will detail in a later chapter. But his stark view of human autonomy is often expressed in terms of "necessity." Necessity isn't limited to external influences. The very choices men make individually or collectively entail a kind of inner compulsion whose consequences can be impossible to reverse.

Much of Florentine history, in Machiavelli's view, centers in the struggle to achieve the overriding goal of virtuous citizens, liberty. A wise citizen is wary of destabilizing an established order for personal aggrandizement, and Machiavelli frequently contrasts such common virtue with the arrogance and brutality of princes. The Florentines at their peak best exemplify the desire for freedom, as when, faced with the growing tyranny of the Duke of Athens, the furious multitude forced him to depart. More often than not, it is the nobles or a prince who wish to enslave the people; occasionally the class roles are reversed. During the struggles in Florence at the turn of the fourteenth and fifteenth centuries, it was the rebellious nobles who tried in vain to rally the populace to throw off the tyranny of Milan. When the conspirators were executed by the Signoria, they realized how risky it is to try to free a people who *want* to be slaves.

With liberty comes unity. Indeed, at least on the rhetorical level, unity may *constitute* liberty. After the death of Frederick II, the Guelfs and Ghibellines were reunited in freedom. When the Duke of Athens was elected as their prince and installed in the Palazzo Vecchio, he invoked the unity of the state in claiming that he was restoring their freedom. Unity is often contrasted with class warfare. Having enjoyed peace and quiet for over thirty years, Florence might have achieved great things if it had remained united and avoided reviving the old "humors" of class. Conversely, during Filippo Visconti's expansion in Lombardy, the Medici were allowed to manipulate these humors in their rise to power, resulting in a decline in citizens' freedom.

At bottom, the struggle for freedom and unity is as much internal as external. In order to thrive, a state must overcome the inherently evil proclivities of men. Machiavelli tends to call this skill "prudence," which alone can overcome the malignity of fortune. The need to contain an evil that both arises from within men and descends from without brings us back to the question of Machiavelli's anthropology, in which men's unstable desires and fears influence their behavior, whether as individuals or collectively. The moral quandaries of such collective decisions exercise him mightily, and he cautions against expecting too much since men always reach for what's beyond their grasp. Thus the plan to kill Lorenzo and Giuliano de' Medici in 1478 faltered when the Pope's *condottiere* balked for lack of courage. But if men's desires exceed their capacities, their hopes exceed their fears. Hence the same Florentines who had opposed fighting Filippo Visconti a year later rushed to attack Lucca, moved more by the hope of acquiring territory than they had been by the fear of losing it. Individually and collectively, men perpetually struggle to know their own minds.

Throughout its history, Florence was roiled by a multitude of passions. Among the greatest of these is the desire for revenge, illustrated by the Ciompi's efforts to enslave their fellow Florentines. In a way, though, the less aggressive impulses can wreak even more havoc. Deceit, for one, can be powerfully destructive, as in the Pazzi Conspiracy of 1478 and Corso Donati's slandering some of his fellow Blacks. Another crucial motive is excessive caution. An early conspiracy of nobles was foiled when the mere perception of danger delayed their proceeding. On balance Machiavelli believes that it's better to settle for half a victory than to risk losing all. However he may admire those who treat fortune roughly like a woman (*The Prince* 25), at the end of the day he is enough of a pragmatist to go with what he knows of the world.

A significant class of evils menaces men organized in states. Here, paradoxically, the wickedness that Machiavelli perceives to be part of the human condition may be exacerbated by the very communalization designed to contain it. The barbarian destruction of the Roman Empire was due as much to the debility of its princes and ministers as to the determination of its attackers. Even more harmful to states of all kinds is a change in their form of government brought about by civil discords, which, as we've seen, cannot be easily reversed.[16] Especially dangerous in this regard are efforts to fashion a city according to some idealized past. Renaissance Rome was especially prey to such nostalgia. When Stefano Porcari sought to liberate Rome from the priests and revive the ancient republic, he was first banished by the Pope and later arrested and killed. While admiring his intentions, Machiavelli concludes that such efforts to restore ancient liberty "have almost always very certain loss in their execution" (VI.29).

Private passions prove especially harmful to the public good. The widespread fear of Corso Donati was so well exploited by his enemies that he was stabbed to death by one of his own men. A similar belief in equality, at least within the dominant class, led the party of the nobles to drive Cosimo and the party of the people out of Florence a few years later. Individual flaws most readily manifest themselves in those occupying positions of authority. After the 1340 conspiracy had been foiled by the people, their leaders were so worked up against the defeated nobles that they were ready to sell the city out. The clash of rival authorities poses a special danger to a state. When Florence was trying to organize itself against Cosimo in 1434, the divided anti-Medici party was disastrously weak in opposing his return from exile.

Perhaps the most severe challenge to a unified authority is the "humors" of class. Contrary to the positive role class division played in the formation of the Roman Republic, in Florence such strife was almost always unhelpful. In contrasting Rome and Florence, Machiavelli acknowledges the "evil" posed by "natural enmities" between the nobility and the people, since the former wish to command and the latter do not wish to obey. But whereas in Rome these enmities led to laws, in Florence they generated conflict; whereas in Rome they enhanced virtue, in Florence they wiped it out; and whereas in Rome they led to a fractious but fruitful inequality, in Florence they effected "a wonderful [*mirabile*: read bizarrely destructive] equality." Finally, whereas in Rome the people's victories improved the entire community, in Florence they merely deprived the nobles of magistracies (III.1).

The worst effect of class is what Machiavelli refers to as "sects." While he concedes that divisions in republics can be fruitful in the public sphere, in private life they are always harmful. The damage caused by class-based sects looms large in Machiavelli's narrative. The internal divisions fostered by the Guelf and Ghibelline noblemen might have been permanently resolved by the latter's banishment. By contrast, the people are motivated less by sectarian considerations than by basic needs. In Machiavelli's view, disunity in Italian cities almost always derives from the aspirations of popes. This pattern was established in the eighth century, when Gregory III called in the French King Pepin II against the dual threat of the emperor and the Langobards. The power of the popes can seem baffling, but even Machiavelli has to concede that their practice of bringing new warriors into Italy and stirring up new wars almost always brought them success.

If the popes were the source of Italian disunity, Florence was its paradigm. Here again Machiavelli can appear flummoxed by the behavior of his ancestors, who often seem bent on self-annihilation. The Florentines can tolerate neither freedom nor slavery, as shown by their conduct under the tyranny of the Duke of Athens. They are especially vulnerable to the evils resulting from peace. The fatal division was that of the ruling Ghibelline party into the Black and White factions, which led to much mischief and brought out the inherent perverseness of the Florentines, who are so susceptible to division that under the Duke of Athens the debt-burdened nobles were even willing to elude their creditors by enslaving their city. Only occasionally have Machiavelli's compatriots displayed a desire for unity and freedom. In the thirteenth century, the Guelfs and Ghibellines briefly reunited after the death of Frederick II. This reconciliation effected a brief golden age in Florentine affairs, the city soared to a new prosperity, and its people found unity in peace.[17]

Machiavelli is under no illusion as to the barriers faced by those trying to achieve an orderly society. In public affairs much rests on minuscule events. Such "accidents" in turn depend on the intrinsic good that wars with the equally intrinsic wickedness of human nature. For Machiavelli this balance of opposites generates a fruitful tension. Both the best and the worst features of our discrete personalities are projected onto the great screen of civic life. Seen in this light, the possibility of good order in the community depends on the marginal advantage held by our better angels in the struggle within each of us. Most men prefer the rule of law to violence and anarchy. This preference allows human collectivities to channel potentially destructive qualities so as to achieve order. Perhaps the most destructive of our motives is competitiveness, which can either generate enmities or lead—as in ancient Rome—to laws, military excellence, and an often productive inequality. Even in its most extreme manifestation, conspiracy, enmity can be turned to the state's or its leader's advantage. Thus, with the city dominated by the Medici, the Florentines had no choice but to resort to conspiracies.

As elsewhere, so also with regard to the complexity of human motives, war raises special considerations. For Machiavelli, at the very least war provides opportunities for glory. When Lucca Pitti ignominiously remained in Florence following its defeat in the 1460s, Machiavelli implicitly disapproves of his choosing to live dishonored among his enemies rather than to die with honor in arms. Similarly, in describing the debate in Florence over how to respond to Filippo Visconti's threat to the city, he emphatically sides with the war party, who argued that fortune favors the attacker over the defender, even though in the sequel Florence was defeated. Naturally, the fortunes of war are chancy because while anyone can start a war, no one can end it. The conduct of war too defies normal logic. Niccolò Piccinino unexpectedly recaptured Verona when he realized that the best chance for success lies with an enterprise your enemy believes to be impossible.

As for modern wars, they mostly strike him as lacking the glamour of their predecessors. Though the aim of modern warfare is to enrich its perpetrators and impoverish its victims, more often than not they have the opposite effect because they are conducted so badly. In Machiavelli's view, the decline in waging war can be attributed almost exclusively to Italian princes' reliance on mercenaries out of distrust of their own subjects. The result is the inglorious avoidance of engagement. In a broad overview of Italy around 1430, he highlights this error. The Pope and the Florentines being for different reasons unarmed, power remained with the *condottieri.* Since these "men without a state" thrived by avoiding battle, "in the end, they reduced [the art of war] to . . . vileness" (I.39).

Vileness is the terminal condition of Florence and Italy as portrayed in the *Florentine Histories.* Despite myriad instances of heroism and a desire for freedom, the overarching assumption in the text is that dormant pettiness and greed have degraded its people to their present reliance on the Medici. Given that the work is dedicated to a Medici Pope, Clement VII, this premise can hardly be developed explicitly. But reading between the lines we can easily arrive at such a conclusion. As Machiavelli understands it, the history of his native land confirms his own fall from political grace, and the ultimate spiritual weakness of Piero Soderini—that faint soul consigned to the limbo of children—encapsulates that of successive generations of Florentines. If *The Prince* records the consequences of Italy's loss of *virtù* and the *Discourses* depicts a state that has retained it, the *Histories* complete Machiavelli's inscription of his political philosophy by documenting those elements in the long story of Florence's decline that reduced it from its former glories to its present ignominy.

CHAPTER 4

MACHIAVELLI AND REPUBLICAN VIRTUE

In the articulation of a viable democratic society, no single word is more central to Machiavellian discourse than *virtue* (*virtù*).[1] *Virtue* has both a political and a philosophical dimension in his works. Indeed, it has both dimensions even in his political works.[2] For while the viability of the state depends on the civic virtue of its citizens, civic virtue in turn rests on individual virtue or integrity—that is, the ability to remain consistently at one with oneself in the face of external threats and conditions. In this chapter, I will focus on Machiavelli's view of the city's dependence on the virtue of individual men; in the next chapter, I'll turn to the philosophical chestnut of virtue versus fortune. Throughout his political and historical writings especially, a controlling premise is that the lack of virtue among his contemporaries contrasts sharply with its abundance in ancient Rome. For example, in the preface to the *Discourses*, Machiavelli claims that contemporary political behavior fails because moderns shun "the virtue of bygone days." It is to remedy this shortcoming that he undertakes his commentary on Livy, explicitly "comparing ancient with modern events."

The foundational concept in Machiavelli's view of civic virtue is "order." The word itself, normally used in the plural, has a somewhat idiosyncratic application in Machiavellian discourse.[3] Basically, it denotes the settled arrangements by which a city conducts its business, for example, "the accustomed orders of his city" that Giovanni de' Medici refuses to upset by joining a conspiracy of noblemen (*F.H.* IV.10). The opposite condition, *disorder*, is a departure from this fundamental order such as mass migration or war. On occasion Machiavelli will use the word synonymously with *practice* or *custom*, as when he speaks of the former "order of sending out colonies," a "custom … eliminated today through the bad practice of republics and princes" (*F.H.* 2.1). Order in this sense is inseparable in Machiavelli's mind from freedom. Hence, after the death of Frederick II, the Florentine Guelfs and Ghibellines were reunited in a "free way of life and … order" (*F.H.* 2.4). Conversely, disorder is associated with chaos and anarchy; thus a disorder that hardens the Black/White division is "the beginning of much evil" (*F.H.* 2.17). Generally, order and disorder take their respective places in a universal pattern, in which order generates virtue, virtue quiet, quiet leisure, leisure disorder, and disorder "ruin."

Order is indispensable to civic virtue. Characteristically, Machiavelli tends to see this issue in terms of form and matter. In discussing corruption in a city, he notes that if one is to impose a "bad form" on a republic, he must first find a "disordered … material" that has evolved over a number of generations (*Disc.* 3.8). Good order is difficult to establish since men are inclined to stick with what they have known. Hence most people are better at preserving a good order than creating one. Broadly speaking, a city has either a good order or a bad one. An exception is modern-day Genoa, which displays a potpourri of liberty and tyranny, civility and corruption, justice and license, "because that order alone keeps the city full of its ancient and venerable customs" (*F.H.* 8.29). More normative are the Romans, who combined order and ardor, whereas the Gauls had ardor but no discipline. On the other hand, if order promotes civic virtue, it can also serve to restrain the destructive tendency of men of *virtù* to push their freedom to the utmost degree, for well-governed individuals do not seek excessive liberty.

Examples of the virtue generated by good order abound in Machiavelli's writings. He insists, for example, that although the personal virtue of citizens is fundamental, favor should be gained by services to the public and not to private individuals. His belief that freedom is prolonged by rewarding good deeds and punishing crimes is qualified by the scandalous axiom that "well-ordered republics have to keep the public rich but their citizens poor" (*Disc.* 1.24). By following this good order, states can achieve or preserve both peace and freedom. Thus, the reunited Florentines refused to make an unprovoked assault on their enemies, whereas the previously ascendant Ghibellines would have abolished every order conducive to freedom. The great modern exemplar of orderly civic virtue is Germany, in whose independent towns citizens pay their taxes without supervision. Conversely, in Italy the feudal conditions of Naples, the Papal States, Romagna, and Lombardy are hostile to any civic order; whereas Florence, Siena, and Lucca, being fortunate enough to lack "gentry," would have a civic constitution if only someone were shrewd enough to introduce one.

Despite the need to preserve it whenever and for as long as possible, order is never a static entity. Apart from the desirability of renewing any order periodically, as the Romans did every ten years, a conscientious reordering of the state is likely to have good consequences. When the Florentine wool-carder Michele di Lando was made gonfalonier following the Ciompi Revolt, he at once proceeded to restore order to the city. Somewhat earlier, the state had similarly been reordered following the expulsion of the Duke of Athens; as a result, the nobles calmed down and for a time Florence remained quiet. Earlier still, after the Ghibelline rout of the Guelfs, it was only when the victors themselves were driven out by the people that the state reordered itself. Yet even a reordered city must perpetually struggle to preserve its gains. Often enough it is the higher-ranking citizens who threaten to upset the applecart. Thus, once order was reestablished in the 1340s, because the nobles lacked the "modesty" demanded by civil life, they were forced to withdraw and the government was again entrusted to the people. The history of these struggles illustrates Machiavelli's conviction that order and civic virtue are essential, mutually reinforcing components of a viable state.

Equally, if not more, compelling is the tension between civic and individual virtue. Here of course we are not speaking of clearly distinguished forces, but rather a subtle orientation of people's inner resources.[4] This is especially problematic for Machiavelli because he believes virtue to be a fundamentally anarchic impulse that drives exceptional men to exert themselves against the world or fortune. Yet this very drive is the guarantor of civic virtue, which implicitly requires individuals to submit their personal will to the interests of the state. It is this reorientation of virtue that distinguishes a healthy from a corrupt city. Even good institutions are not good in a corrupt state, where power seekers preclude men of virtue from exercising power. As restoring political life requires such men, it's impossible to fashion or maintain a republican form of government in corrupt states.

The virtue of exceptional individuals contributes in many ways to the civic virtue necessary to reorder and maintain states. As usual, the prime exemplar is ancient Rome, where the builders' virtue was reflected in the city's fortune. The Romans exercised their virtue by promulgating laws, and those issued by Romulus in turn amplified the city's already abundant virtue. Therefore, Romulus's successors relied upon their own virtue to maintain a viable state. Machiavelli is somewhat ambivalent as to whether the Roman emperors in general manifested outstanding virtue. Though he singles out Severus as a man whose virtue gave him stature in the eyes of his people and soldiery, Severus's successors lacked the virtue to follow his example. In contemporary Italy, Francesco Bussone, the Count of Caramagnola, led the Venetians successfully against the Duke of Milan. Some of Machiavelli's heroes demonstrate their virtue by what they don't do. Rinaldo degli Albizzi failed to enlist Giovanni de' Medici in the conspiracy of nobles to overthrow the established order in Florence. In Milan, Galeazzo Sforza lacked the virtue of his father Francesco to rally opposition to the rising Lorenzo de' Medici in Florence a year after his grandfather Cosimo's death.

For various reasons, not all virtuous men successfully channel their personal virtue into the well-being of the community. Sometimes this is simply a question of circumstances. For example, Hiero of Syracuse could not fulfill his considerable virtue without a kingdom to rule, and even Theseus could not have manifested his without the Athenians' confusion. In other instances, the leader's *virtù* is not accompanied by virtue. Among the ancients, Hannibal's cruelty made him feared; absent this cruelty, his other virtues would have failed, as evidenced by Scipio, who had all the other requisite virtues to succeed. But the most egregious example is Agathocles the Sicilian, who applied his abundant virtues to the committing of many crimes. While conceding that it cannot be called "virtue" to murder one's fellow citizens, Machiavelli insists that if we take into consideration only Agathocles's *virtù*, he could certainly be called great. The moderns are no less subject to the whims of chance. Agathocles's modern counterpart is Cesare Borgia, whose virtuosity was so great that he might have united Italy by the sheer force of his *virtù* had his father the Pope lived a bit longer. On the other hand, the Florentines were sometimes fortunate because the leaders of virtue they had reason to fear were not always victorious.

Whether and how this kind of virtue impinges on the city is a difficult call. Certainly, any civic leader must be willing to acknowledge the virtue of others. Machiavelli points out that either fear, as in the case of Hannibal, or kindness, as with Scipio, works if one has virtue, and both can be harmful if he does not. Thus the soldiers mutinied against Scipio in Spain, while fear of Hannibal kept the surrounding towns loyal to Rome. In any case, war itself is of such virtue that it benefits princes and private citizens alike. Yet despite his conventional association of virtue with outstanding individuals, for the arch-republican Machiavelli, civic virtue resides preeminently with the people. Princes may excel at instituting new laws, but the populace achieves even greater renown by maintaining them. Hence there is more virtue in the people than in their prince.

For this reason, the value of a civilization should be judged by its *collective* virtue. Even in his own day, though Italian military virtue has fled, yet "the limbs of the nation have great *virtù*" (*Pr.* 26). Among the ancients, the Ostrogoth leader Theodoric's complaint to the Eastern Emperor Zeno that his virtuous people lacked an empire prevailed, and Zeno allowed Theodoric to take over Italy. Similarly, it was the Florentines' ability to uphold their reputation for civic virtue that allowed them to reorder their city after expelling the Ghibellines in the thirteenth century. These examples show that the stellar acts of leaders of virtue frequently reflect the superior civic virtue of the people they lead. In times of international strife, one's natural concern for the welfare of the state may arouse the best instincts of individuals or at least restrain their worst ones. In the most somber of Machiavelli's Carnival Songs, the Blessed Spirits, having descended from heaven to warn Italy against continuing the war between France and the Empire, beg their listeners to exchange fear for love of honor and virtue.[5]

Finally, if the virtue of individuals endues a city with civic virtue, the latter can also reinforce personal virtue. In one of the more philosophical passages of *L'Asino*, Machiavelli projects a typical panorama of fortune's ceaseless motion, in which good and evil perpetually succeed each other. In this eternal order of things, virtue imposes peace on regions, which generates leisure, which soon destroys the land. From these disorders, however, in time virtue arises to inhabit the land again. The whole cycle of virtue/tranquility/leisure/ruin/disorder/virtue is comprehended under the aegis of "Order," and this order-in-change is directed by "Him who governs us" (*Asino*, Capitolo 5).[6] In the poem, this historical-political order repeats the personal one suffered by the narrator and explicated by the Lady in an earlier chapter. But whereas states cannot escape the cycle because men of ambition, greed, and power will always supply the virtue that fuels it, individuals can transcend it by capitalizing on the opportunity provided by their personal misfortune to understand its universal laws. Only on the philosophical level, that is, can the individual escape the vicious cycle that constrains historical events.

For Machiavelli, who spent many of his most productive days in the boondocks raising and training militia, the most important species of civic virtue is military virtue. So central is this premise to his civic outlook that at times one feels that for him there is little to distinguish military virtue from simply virtue. At its most extreme, this bias expresses itself in a quasi-glorification of war, and even of death. His claim, for example, that the victory of the Pope's forces over the Milanese near Rome in the 1480s was "fought with more virtue" than any other in half a century is based solely on the fact that the battle cost the lives of more than a thousand men (*F.H.* 8.23). Likewise, only excellence on the battlefield can sustain national honor. It was the virtue of the Romagnese company of St. George in 1400, for example, that reclaimed for Italy a reputation for excellence in arms.

In Machiavelli's mind, military virtue is the natural complement to laws. He never tires of yoking laws and arms as the dual cornerstones of a city's reputation. A city may be a paragon of civic virtue and mutual respect in the conduct of its day-to-day functions; yet if it is not able to defend itself, or to come when called upon to the aid of its allies, it will soon lose the respect of its neighbors and become prey to its enemies. At the same time, Machiavelli is tentative about how military virtue bears on the course of events in a city's history. In contrasting the diverse effects of natural hostility between people and nobles, he notes that in Rome they increased military virtue whereas in Florence they eliminated it. Hence, Rome acquired more virtue from the people's victories, while Florence saw the opposite result, especially among its nobility.

Finally, religious virtue has a complicated relation to military virtue and to virtue in general. Not only does religion play a major role in maintaining order in a state, but it can be invoked to create an aura of power, a sustaining mystique that will propel men into battle. At one point Machiavelli recalls how the Romans employed auguries and auspices to inspire confidence in the mettle of their general. The generals, for their part, would never omit these rituals before entering battle and would be severely punished if they did. Nevertheless, Machiavelli insists that these practices are worthless without virtue. His assertion that the Samnites' "virtue of religion" succumbed to "the virtue of the Romans" leads us to suspect that Machiavelli harbors a somewhat utilitarian view of the role of religion in human affairs (*Disc.* 1.15). So long as a military body is composed of men of virtue, religious conviction can only strengthen its resolve in battle; but the absence of such a belief, like the absence of a leader, will not deter a virtuous army.

For Machiavelli, virtue is a fundamental component of human nature. Indeed, it is so basic to all social activities that it trumps virtually all other considerations. In exploring the consequences of Rome's opening the consulate to the plebs, Machiavelli notes that they also removed any criterion of age or birth, seeking only virtue whether in the young or the old. He cites approvingly the example of Valerius Corvinus, who was appointed consul at age twenty-three as "the reward of virtue, not of birth." If the public, he comments, knows of a young man who has performed well and still denies him a prominent position in the city, the failure to avail itself of his virtue till he has lost his "vigor" will inevitably cause harm to the city (*Disc.* 1.60).

Machiavelli's vocabulary here implies that *virtù* may have an erotic component. This is clearly the case in *L'Asino* when the narrator first meets the lady who will revive his flagging powers. In the second chapter, the critical moment in their sexual encounter seems designed to echo Machiavelli's delivery from the Medici prison. At the very moment when he succumbs to her charms, the lady restores his virtue with her amorous innuendoes. The consequence of his revival will be a Dantean descent into the underworld, whose reward will be the sanction to castigate those who have been the agents of his own misfortunes. When, on the verge of this descent, the lady is compelled to chide him for his lack of virtue, her words quickly revive it. Like his compression of Dante's journey into a single descent into an erotic paradise, and his fusion of Vergil and Beatrice into a sole guide who is also his sexual partner, his use of *virtù* in these passages underscores its eroticization in *L'Asino*.

More generally, Machiavellian virtue is a mysterious quantity whose function seems dicey. For example, following the death of Cosimo de'

Medici, the Florentines held a tournament at a festival, at which the young Lorenzo seemingly came from nowhere to win top honors. When Francesco Sforza's son and successor as Duke of Milan, Galeazzo, sought continuation of the tribute Florence had been paying to Milan, those Florentines opposing the payments argued that the alliance had been made with Francesco, not Galeazzo, and that there was no reason to renew it because Galeazzo lacked his father's virtue. Such examples make clear the extent to which political decisions are routinely made on the basis, or calculation, of individual virtue.

Its complex social ramifications work variously for good or ill. On the one hand, personal virtue can strengthen political relations within a city, as when Giovanni de' Medici declined to conspire to seize power in Florence. On the other hand, the lack of virtue can impel men in power to do foolish and even self-defeating things. Jacopo Piccinino's virtue compelled Francesco Sforza to have King Ferdinand kill him in Naples. As Machiavelli comments, "So much did our Italian princes fear in others the virtue that was not in themselves" (*F.H.* 7.8). Finally, in the dedication of his *Histories*, Machiavelli alludes ambiguously to the virtue of the natural son left behind by Giuliano de' Medici in 1516.[7]

Central as it is to Machiavelli's thinking about politics and government, virtue is not always treated with either consistency or clarity. One of the most puzzling and recurring paradoxes concerns the role of "necessity" in the formation of virtue. At the outset of his history of Florence, Machiavelli praises the virtue of those who found cities. Yet he immediately goes on to argue that such virtue is more a product of necessity than of choice. For example, the very idleness fostered by fertile locales imposed the need for the Romans to exercise virtue by establishing the rule of law. Similarly, he argues that since "virtue … lies in necessity," a prudent general should always contrive to make it necessary for his own troops to do battle (*Disc.* 3.12).

To digress briefly, apart from its relation to virtue, Machiavelli's scattered observations on necessity provide an important insight into his sometimes erratic thinking. Some of these remarks are implicitly negative, while a larger number seem at best neutral. The negative examples are the most intriguing, as their presentation usually claims to be positive. Thus in contrasting the Romans' gratitude to their citizens with the Athenians' apparent lack of it, Machiavelli explains that one should ascribe both Athens' depriving its people of liberty and Rome's failure to do so to the necessities of their respective circumstances. Less ambiguous is the explanation of why entire peoples abandon their own countries to occupy others'. Making a distinction between wars of "ambition" and those of "necessity," Machiavelli surprisingly argues that the latter—that is, those brought on by famine, war, or hardships in their own land—are more cruel and dangerous because whole populations are threatened or replaced, and that those who wage them are therefore hard to resist (*Disc.* 2.8).

If these examples show Machiavelli exerting little effort to make a virtue of necessity, others reveal an underlying ambivalence. Here we may suspect the kind of fatalism that will come into play when we turn to his conjectures on *virtù* and *fortuna*. A few instances betray genuine neutrality. In relating how the Romans broadened the classes of citizens admitted to high offices, he observes that once the plebs had been included, ignoring age and birth was a good practice even if it was done out of necessity. In another discourse, Machiavelli cynically submits that a republic or prince should claim to be doing out of "generosity" what is in fact dictated by necessity. Thus, the Roman Senate paid its army with public money since it couldn't wage wars on its own nickel.

Other instances suggest a more positive spin. Machiavelli describes with evident approval how when Lucca was abandoned by Filippo Visconti, an elder persuaded them to defend their city by justifying acts performed out of necessity. In a similar vein, Francesco Sforza, realizing that he has been made a fool of in agreeing to marry the daughter of Filippo Visconti, reconciles himself to the decision because it had been taken out of necessity. Among the ancients, the Romans wisely bowed to necessity in allowing the subject Latins and Hernici to conduct their own defense when they themselves were unable to do it. By contrast, Florence stubbornly resisted necessity in refusing Cesare Borgia passage through its territory in 1501 and distrusting France with respect to Pisa in 1500 and Arezzo in 1502.

If these examples show Machiavelli making a virtue of necessity, his more typical arguments promote the necessity of virtue. Whereas Machiavelli typically conceptualizes virtue as locked in a perpetual struggle with fortune, in a new city the degree of virtue of its founder or builder is generative of, and therefore reflected in, its fortune. This is manifest in both the choice of a site and the institution of laws, as for example Aeneas' virtue is observable in the achievements of Troy. Whatever the sources of a city's virtue, it tends to reduce disputes about such questions as the means of waging war. For example, in a time of transition from feudal to modern technological warfare, arguments abounded as to whether guns, especially large cannon, are honorable means of inflicting harm on the enemy. But Machiavelli rejects the argument that artillery precludes virtue by preventing hand-to-hand fights and hence personal conquest, concluding that it can be "useful" if sustained by virtue but remains "useless if not" (*Disc.* 2.17).

Machiavelli consistently views Italian history through the lens of virtue. Compared with ancient Roman virtue, that history is little more than a continuously dismal decline. In the *Histories*, at the point in his narrative where Cosimo is about to return from exile and establish Medici hegemony in Florence, the author pauses to frame this crucial moment. Stepping back from the narrative flow of events, Machiavelli indulges in a protracted reflection on historical change in which the whole span of Medici hegemony, roughly 1434–1494, is characterized as one of "virtue ... eliminated by vileness" (*F.H.* 4.33). This account is tendentious throughout. Anticipating the catastrophes that occurred under the Medici, Machiavelli speculates that such dismal modern things may be as useful to the reader as the brighter ones of the ancients because if the latter inspire imitation, the former may encourage avoidance. In this rare, if oblique, characterization of the reader of the *Histories*, Machiavelli drops the disguise of a disinterested historian virtually required by the work's Medicean ambiance in order to signal its larger patriotic purpose. The chapter's structure bears out this strategy. Machiavelli's standard cyclical view of history, in which states normally progress from order to disorder and back to order again, is analogized with that from virtue to quiet to leisure to ruin, and again to virtue, glory, and good fortune. Moreover, in the evolution from virtue to ruin, arms gradually give way to letters, and captains to philosophers, in an ironic descent whose unspoken name is corruption. Though the remnants of the Roman Empire failed to build upon its noble ruins, yet some of the emerging cities were able to work together to defend Italy from the "barbarians" without any one of them dominating the others and forming an empire. The result was a kind of imperial limbo, in which these discrete states were suspended between the corrosive *otium* of peace and the perilous strife of war. Somewhere in between, Italy loses its virtue through a protracted series of minor skirmishes. The sequel is the infamy of Medici dominance about to be narrated, in which Italy succumbs to a willing "slavery" to the "barbarians" (*F.H.* 5.1).

Machiavelli tries valiantly, and possibly ironically, to exempt pre-Medicean Florence from this blistering condemnation. When the Guelfs and Ghibellines were temporarily reunified, the reorganized city once more enjoyed a period of peace and stability. But when the conflict was renewed under Manfred and the victorious Ghibellines abolished freedom, the people once again drove them out of the city and reestablished the rule of law and arms, only to have Pope Gregory X excommunicate the city because the Ghibellines feared to return. And so it went until now Ghibelline Florence further divided into Blacks and Whites, the Whites (including Dante) were banished, the ruling Blacks fell into factions, the Duke of Athens intervened, and so on down to the rivalry of the Albizzi and the Medici and the latter's dominance in Machiavelli's own time. As his prefatory framings make abundantly clear, in contrast to the social fertility of such internecine struggles in Rome, the ultimate product of these "enmities" in Florence was not an expansive imperial republic, but Medici hegemony.

It seems appropriate to end this anatomy of Machiavellian virtue with its bitterly satiric deconstruction at the end of *L'Asino*. In this narrative poem, a deliberate parody of Dante's *Commedia* is fused with the metamorphosis motif of Apuleius' *Golden Ass*. Although it is evidently unfinished—in its preamble he clearly refers to a physical transformation that never occurs in the text as we have it—it begins when a Beatrice-like lady rescues the narrator from a dark valley where he is surrounded by beasts who were once men. After entertaining him with a sumptuous meal and a night of love, the lady promises to redeem him with her gift of illumination. In his disguise, the narrator enters the "dormitory" where the lady's mistress Circe harbors her bestial wards. At its far end, a door swings open to reveal thousands of beasts, many of whom the narrator vaguely recognizes, terminating in a fat pig wallowing in his muddy "den." Approaching the pig, he recognizes the man beneath his bestial mask and offers at once to help him escape. As the lady has predicted, the pig leaps up and, vehemently refusing the offer, delivers a tirade.

The tenor of his speech is signaled at the outset as not so much a self-defense as an accusation of the narrator himself. Accusing the latter of being deluded by "self-love," he launches into a conventional naturalistic praise of the superior life of animals. Beginning with prudence, he proclaims that he and the other animals are endowed with all the human virtues that give men their supposed superiority. But these virtues come to them by instinct and not from any mentor. More tellingly, unlike humans they exercise them without any desire for praise or renown. Men, on the other hand, out of greed and ambition pervert their endowment and immodestly give all to the service of their cruder senses. As a result, they are unhappier than the animals. The latter, therefore, are closer to Nature, who is pleased to give them most of her virtues, leaving men with empty hands.

Even the virtues with which men *are* endowed work to their disadvantage. Perhaps the only exception to Nature's favoring the beasts over men in the sensory realm is the latter's sense of touch. But this has proven to be a kind of Pandora's Box in that it was only intended to increase men's sense of shame. Similarly, she gave men the gift of speech, but then neutralized it by adding ambition and greed, "distress" and lust. Yet no other animal has a more precarious existence, and none is fraught by a desire to live so mingled with fear and rage. Afflicted with such passions, men alone murder, crucify, and rob each other, while their bestial brethren live in peace, content with what they have. Given such blatant differences, the pig is more than satisfied to renounce a life of human suffering and stay where he is. Warning the narrator to be wary of anyone claiming to be as happy as himself, he ends by reaffirming his "carefree" life rolling in the mud. There he will remain happy among the other noble beasts.

Here both chapter and poem end. But to a certain extent the pig's teaching deconstructs the narrator's own earlier meditation in see Chapter 5 on the appetite for fame and material goods that drives men. There, after rescuing the narrator from his torpor in the dark wood, the accommodating handmaid of Circe lures him to her bed. At first he cowers under a blanket, but under her cunning hands his "virtue" quickly revives and their love-feast commences. With the coming of dawn, the narrator is temporarily left alone in her room. Reflecting on his own change of fortune, he lets his thoughts wander to the vicissitudes of nations.

The explanation, he finds, lies in men's irreversible drive for power. Anticipating the pig's critique a few chapters later, our meditator reflects on the cycle of motives that governs worldly events. As the virtues of rivals clash, the winners get to indulge their appetites while the losers are left wallowing in their desire for revenge. This pattern is displayed in the history of Venice, Athens, Sparta, and Germany, and it now fits the behavior of Florence, which, when it was content to remain confidently strong within its walls, was safe even from the threat of a Henry VII, but, now that it has expanded its reach, is fearful of everything. Here Machiavelli is equivocal about such expansiveness. Understanding that in cities, as in men, the virtue that causes one to overreach is a praiseworthy innate force—a fact of nature—he must distinguish between the thing itself and its excess. The attempt to do so is both interesting and confusing. And though the chapter ends with a forthright condemnation of pious fatalists who would rely on God to reward their prayers and fasting with worldly success, one is left with the distinct impression that the reasons for worldly change are ultimately unknowable. In short, while virtue plays a key role in determining the fate of cities, in the final analysis the reasons they rise or fall remain a mystery.

To pursue Machiavelli's argument further, we might pick it up where he acknowledges Florence's current state of fear. By way of explanation he observes that the personal virtue that suffices to sustain a single body fails when it attempts to bear more. It's true, he reasons, that a state will survive to the degree that it has good laws and order. A principality compelled to function as either virtue or necessity dictates will always rise in power, whereas one that lacks such motivators will be subject to change, oscillating between good laws and bad behavior. At this juncture we might expect some speculation as to what differentiates the always-rising powers from those doomed to a cyclical rise and fall. Instead, we get the formulaic and essentially fatalistic anatomy of virtue, tranquility, laziness, disorder, and renewed virtue already cited. In that passage Machiavelli's persona attributes the cycle to an omnipotent God who wills the eternal exchange of good and evil. Though some believe that the greed or lust that topple nations may be overcome by prayers, fasting, and alms, the narrator demurs. Prayers may be "necessary," and religion properly harnessed brings a city "order" and "good fortune," but he dismisses as foolish anyone who would wait for God to rescue him from his collapsing house.

Projected onto the world scene, this fatalistic fantasy would seem to situate the narrator at the opposite pole from Machiavelli. Here virtue alone would seem to be all that is required for an individual or a city to avoid its fate. Yet such self-determination has already been reduced to the inalterable cycle of good and evil, order and chaos, virtue and moral flaccidity, perpetuated by an all-governing deity. In his private reflections on the fate of nations in Chapter 3, the narrator-hero of *L'Asino* demonstrates the intellectual quandary that will render him susceptible to the sardonic persuasions of the misanthropic pig. Between these two poles, Machiavelli's fragmentary satire leaves the reader pondering whether all human striving for excellence and fame is merely a perversion of nature.

Apart from *L'Asino* and some of his shorter poems, Machiavelli's literary works are less inclined to anatomize virtue than to dramatize it. Yet in his minor poems there are a few scattered passages that contribute to our understanding of its centrality in his thinking. As always, its effect radiates outward from the virtuous individual. For example, early in the second *Decennale*, Machiavelli heaps praise on the Florentine commissioner, Antonio Giacomini, who earned unprecedented fame by overcoming a renegade *condottiere*. Such an emphasis on a self-generated virtue is rare in the poems, possibly because their genre demands a more cosmic orientation. In praising Savonarola's virtue, for example, he describes the heroic monk as "spurred by divine breath of virtue," a phrase that evenly distributes it between himself and heaven (*Dec.* 1.158). Similarly, his "Pastoral Chapter" can simultaneously grant the mythical Hyacinth personal virtues while attributing them to "Heaven," which chose to display its own virtue in him.

The ambiguity in Machiavelli's presentation of Hyacinth's virtue brings us, as always, to the blurred margins of the self and the other. But even where he focuses on virtue alone, Machiavelli can fudge what on the surface would seem to be a clear distinction. An example is the short poem "Di fortuna," written in 1512, whose very title implies a fatalistic contextualization of virtue. The poem begins by positing virtue as the sole barrier to fortune's power, but it goes on to raise the prickly question of our beliefs regarding the goods we achieve in our lives. At one point the poem's speaker accuses the reader of blaming fortune for his faults while attributing his successes to his own virtue. A bit later, this delusion is corrected by ascribing to the heavens an irrational *virtù* that denies us the power to control our own fortunes. This rejection of autonomous virtue is even stronger in the slightly later "Ambition" (1516), where men's efforts to achieve what they deem to be good are reduced to "oppressing" this or that rather than exercising their own virtue. Only in Paradise, it seems, can men—their worldly substance now sublimated—unambiguously proclaim that their essential "virtue" lives forever ("The Blessed Spirits").

As we have come to expect, it is with regard to military virtue that Machiavelli is least ambivalent. The irresistible force of military virtue is summed up best in "Ambition." Rhetorically posing the question why some nations dominate others—specifically, why France rules while Italy cringes—when ambition reigns in every land, he attributes the difference to virtue, which renders the individual immune to the mental afflictions of fear. When, in addition, a community of such individuals has been licked into order by good laws, the fury with which its ambition hurls itself against external enemies is irresistible. These instances give us a sense of the force of virtue in driving men to arms and states to aggressive conduct against their neighbors. But it is his comedies, and especially his masterpiece *Mandragola*, that best enact, if they do not indeed parody, the concept of civic virtue and its relation with or derivation from that of the individual.

Explicit references to virtue in *Mandragola* are few and, except in the prologue, trivial. In Act II, Scene 2, Callimaco flatters the doltish Nicia that men like him are "virtuous," a compliment that is echoed by Nicia himself in the following scene, where he reflects that virtue like his own is not appreciated in the corrupt Florence of his day.[8] But, in the prologue the author's persona situates himself in a veritable minidrama of fallen civic virtue in the guise of a mock apology for his unworthy material. Banned by his personal fate from displaying other virtues in other ways, he claims to have adopted perforce the role of scourge of his epoch, meeting the expected public criticism of his efforts in kind by "speaking ill." Since his audience in turn is hampered by a general lack of civic virtue from appreciating and rewarding his efforts, the author's and the audience's "speaking ill" are locked in a vicious cycle that he accepts in lieu of praise.

I will return for a fuller discussion of the play in Chapter 6. But though the word itself occurs only rarely, the concept of virtue is a key to its action. And because the motor of this action is the parasite-figure

Ligurio, I will focus my attention on this character as a possible bearer of its value. While the protagonists of his more conventional comedies bear out Machiavelli's existential privileging of men (and women) of "character" whose virtue implies a stable self, it is the manipulative trickster Ligurio who serves as the model of Machiavellian virtue in the play.[9]

We should be wary of being too quick to dismiss Ligurio as a mere animator of events. While it is true that his power to control others' reality constitutes his virtuosity as a con man, Ligurio embodies the quintessentially Machiavellian ideal of *virtù* as disinterested amorality. He seems to stand totally outside the events he is orchestrating; yet his complex and guarded motivation includes an insidious ability to enter into others' psyches. The key to understanding the play may lie in the elusive mandragola itself. This token is more than merely "a word without substance" by whose virtue "people can be manipulated rhetorically to believe in" another's reality.[10] Rather, Callimaco's potion is emblematic of the mysterious self, mirroring each character's beliefs, desires, and blindnesses; in short, of *virtù*. On those who control it, however, it bestows the gift of self-knowledge, sharing the power of the lady in *L'Asino*. It is an elixir for the knowing that underscores the unique virtues of the literary imagination. Inoculated by reality, its true master is immune to its destructive power. By this final metamorphosis of *L'Asino*'s metaphoric *medicina* to the symbolic *mandragola*, our author transcends his personal misfortune to produce at last an exemplar of Machiavellian virtue.

In contrast to the subtly ironic *Mandragola*, *Clizia* straightforwardly invests the values of *virtù* in its female protagonist, Sofronia. Her chief function in the play is to restore her husband Nicomaco to what she calls the "arrangement of his life" (2.4).[11] Faced with ruin and anarchy, Sofronia and the other women are armed with virtue in the form of superior wit. In the face of Nicomaco's dereliction, Machiavelli transfers legitimate moral authority, that is, civic virtue, to his wife. In contrast to the centered Sofronia, not only the love-blinded Nicomaco, but even the young hero Cleandro is reduced to impotent passivity because he lacks her virtue. Torn between his parents' warring aims for dispensing of Clizia, he finds his natural virtue at war with his desires, at one point lamenting that fortune is in this case, and unnaturally, the friend of the old. Even the dénouement, brought about by the surprise appearance of Clizia's father, Ramondo, serves only to reinforce Sofronia's virtue. For it is not Ramondo's character, but merely the news he bears, that authorizes the plot's resolution. The moral authority rests with Sofronia and her "correcting" her husband's abandonment of his self.

By this surprising investment in the feminine as the locus of virtue, Machiavelli appears in historical retrospect to redeem *virtù* from the connotation of mere virtuosity. Even more tellingly, this shift in gender constitutes an implicit abandonment of his own claim to virtue. Where *Mandragola* emphatically identifies its virtuosic protagonist with the author himself, in the *Clizia* Machiavelli implicitly identifies himself with the play's wayward, and ultimately "corrected," butt ("Nicomaco" = Niccolo Machiavelli). In effect, his second and last original comedy cancels out his first by constructing a female protagonist who fuses the virtuosity of prestidigitation with substantive virtue. Implicitly, the virtue that Sofronia reimposes on the on-stage community has the capacity to render its citizens truly virtuous. Hence her personal virtue satisfies the Machiavellian paradigm by generating civic virtue as well.

CHAPTER 5

MACHIAVELLI AND THE REALM OF FORTUNE

Opposing virtue as the key to preserving freedom in civic life is the role of fortune in human affairs. In a sense, by turning from *virtù* to *fortuna* we are simply abandoning the political for the philosophical realm. For many late-medieval thinkers (Lorenzo Valla is an example) there is no inconsistency in believing that while all our acts are governed by forces beyond our control, we are nevertheless autonomous agents free at any given moment to choose one course of action over another.[1] Similarly, for Machiavelli, while individuals may exercise their innate abilities to shape their personal and collective outcomes, the role of fortune in human affairs ranges over a wide spectrum.

At times Machiavelli writes as a fatalist who believes that fortune holds total sway. Even the penultimate chapter of *The Prince*, a text notorious for embracing the opposite view, begins with his announcement that he himself "incline[s] toward" the "popular" view that men are helpless against the rule of fortune (*Pr.* 25). In the *Discourses* he often seems on the verge of conceding an impenetrable ceiling on the exercise of human freedom. Occasionally, he invokes Livy to buttress this superstition without quite disassociating himself from his source. For example, he quotes without comment Livy's observation that "fortune blind[s] the minds of men when she does not want them to oppose [her] force" (*Disc.* 2.30), then tacitly endorses the historian's view that fortune prevented the Romans from buying their safety from the Gauls. Later he argues that if one conforms one's conduct to the flow of events, one's fortune will thrive.

Sometimes this quasi-fatalistic view of fortune's reign seems little more than a verbal reflex. In the *Florentine Histories* he observes that fortune often couples one good or evil with another. But elsewhere in the same work there is no such equivocation, as when he proclaims the extraordinary fall of Jacopo di Messer Poggio "a very great example of fortune" (*F.H.* 8.9). Likewise, in the *Decennali* he affirms that it was the fortune of Siena, Genoa, and Lucca to be defeated by Venice, and in the letter to Gianbattista Soderini known as the *Ghiribizzi*, he concludes that fortune alone controls men's outcomes. His most equivocal utterance on the ultimate order of things comes in *L'Asino*, where the effect of virtue is attributed to *chi ci governa*, which can be translated as either "Him who" or "that which governs us." Equivocation dissolves into caricature in *Clizia*, where the doltish Nicomaco recommends submitting the issue of who gets the girl to fortune in the form of a bag of ballots.[2] The play's putative hero Cleandro doesn't come off much better when he observes of a momentary setback that "fortune [has thrown him] back into the middle of the sea" just when he thought he'd made it to port.

At the opposite pole from this fatalism is the precept that as free agents men can dominate fortune. In general, Machiavelli appears to be an optimist who believes that by taking precautions we can improve our chances of overcoming fortune.[3] This view is set forth in the penultimate chapter of *The Prince*, which addresses "The Influence of Luck (*fortuna*) on Human Affairs" (*Pr.* 25). Having chided Italian princes for "blam[ing] fortune" rather than "their own sloth" for their loss of power (*Pr.* 24), he now concedes that "Fortune governs half our actions." Deploying a metaphor of flood control to support the idea that "she leaves the other half" to us, he asserts that though fortune's torrents may wreak havoc on the countryside, once the storm has passed men can shore up their defenses with dikes and dams. He ends the chapter by famously invoking the figure of the young stud asserting his mastery of the feminine. Men will flourish or flounder according to "the times," but "Fortune is a woman," "a friend of the young" to be mastered by brute strength (*Pr.* 25).[4]

This stout young man is the prototype of the fortune-subduing Machiavellian hero. In the peroration to *The Prince*, such a swashbuckling posture is somewhat ludicrously recommended to the Medici. Picking up the slack from Cesare Borgia, who was abandoned by fortune at the top of his game, this "illustrious house" is well positioned to reverse Italy's misfortunes (*Pr.* 26). But the *Discourses* provide more persuasive examples—perhaps because they come from the Roman past—as well as contrasting negative ones from present-day Italy. The latter include the Venetians, whose good fortune derived from a specious appearance of virtue. The Roman counter-example is Camillus. Whereas lesser men are inflated by good fortune but collapse when the pendulum swings against them, men like Camillus stay on an even keel. And because they never change, anyone can see that they are immune to fortune's slings and arrows. Against the array of exemplars of fortune's absolute dominance of human affairs, Machiavelli poses these mythical and historical autonomous heroes.

Even his most aggressive formulations of human autonomy usually hint at some mental reservation. Machiavelli's briefs for human mastery of events are almost always qualified by an awareness of whimsical forces of history and fortune.[5] He is equally aware of the quixotic nature of men's efforts to resist these ruinous forces: it is the *illusion* of virtue that drives his heroes. Working against these thrusts of the ego are the quirky chances that inform his fantastic vision of human life and the poetic language in which he records it. Even in *The Prince* his great exemplars of virtue are always defeated, so that one may legitimately doubt the possibility of achieving any but the briefest triumph over the forces of disorder. Hence the second half of the work, with its emphasis on reputation and the reflected nature of the self, undercuts the implicit thesis of its first half that success is achievable through individual effort. To conquer the forces of ruin, the best one can hope for is to control appearances. It's the art of the latter that emerges as the supreme virtue, and the man most able to hold power on the stage of history is the one who is best at manipulating appearances. Even a Cesare Borgia is at maximum efficacy when he arranges to present the spectacle of Remiro de Orca as tyrant and himself as tyrannicide and redeemer of the oppressed.

Between these two poles, Machiavelli records a rainbow of responses to fortune's reign. At various times he defines fortune as sometimes "a causal agent," sometimes "fortuitous events," and sometimes "a favourable or unfavourable condition of life."[6] One posture stresses the capacity of the individual to calculate, or even collaborate with, her will. Here the underlying premise is that fortune cannot be controlled but only complied with. Thus, in launching an argument for adaptability, Machiavelli begins by conceding that "men are sometimes unfortunate, sometimes fortunate." This premise dictates that individuals can "second" but not "oppose" their fortune or, more graphically, that "they may weave its warp, but cannot break it" (*Disc.* 3.9). Even so, they should never stop resisting their fortune. Although one's destination is rarely clear, "there is always hope," and hope will conquer regardless of fortune (*Disc.* 2.29). Machiavelli's writings are shot through with similar predications of the limited freedom accorded men in their struggle for autonomous agency in a world of chance.

The individual's ability to collaborate with fortune is often seen as an opportunity, or even a challenge. And it prompts metaphors both more subtle and more empowering than that of weaving oneself into her warp. In a long letter to Vettori in 1514 in which he assumes the posture of the Pope assessing events in Europe, Machiavelli rephrases the situation in terms of fortune. Given the uncertainty of her activities, what should a wise man do? The answer is "draw close to" the fortune that will lead to the least bad result. At this point in the spectrum of human freedom, the best Machiavelli can imagine is a sort of modest sidling up to the fortune that promises the least bad result (*L.* 243). But not all collaborators with fortune are so passively constrained. Kings are virtually immune to her swings, or at least so some French monarchists assert. In any case, individuals, like communities, can always exercise their relative freedom by rolling the dice. This is especially true of armies and their leaders, who, he asserts three times, can always "try [their] luck in battle" (*Disc.* 3.41). Lacking supplies, generals must either fight or succumb to hunger. Choosing to fight in these circumstances not only displays honor, but allows fortune the chance to bestow favor. The implication is that just as fortune can sometimes provide the occasion for men to act freely, so individuals may act in a way that gives her the opportunity to reciprocate.

How one relates to the less fortunate is a key marker of one's own virtue. In discussing how a ruler wins friends, Machiavelli underscores the loss of credibility entailed in not coming to the support of a loser. If you are not willing to throw in your lot with him, he is unlikely to do the same when your respective fortunes are reversed. On the other hand, if you do support him in bad times, he will stick with you when your own fortune turns. In all these instances, while the chance to operate as a free agent may be constrained by unfavorable circumstances, they never shut one out completely. Indeed, the narrowness of one's choice only enhances the value of choosing. The more one's fortune fluctuates, the greater the opportunity to assert one's freedom and virtue by electing to act.

The nobler option of floating above fortune's realm existed only for the ancient Romans. At first they had no knowledge of her instability, but this desirable state turns out to have concealed a vulnerability: being thus unprepared for fortune's changes, they quickly succumbed to avarice, ambition, and rapine, and their democracy soon devolved into oligarchy. The fullest exposition of the Roman ideal comes around once again to the ascendancy of virtue over fortune. Because they were well armed and well disciplined, the Romans were able to test both their virtue and their fortune in action, invariably passing with flying colors. Those with less martial prowess are subject wholly to fortune and will always and inevitably follow her whims.

In Machiavelli's more pragmatic moods, the lofty Roman ideal remains outside of men's capacities, and he exhorts us to shift with fortune's changes. The capitolo *Fortune* attributes to fortune the desire that we alter with her alterations.[7] Equally lyrical, though in prose, is Machiavelli's passionate argument in the *Ghiribizzi* that one must "try Fortune [and] change according to the times." Speculating as to why the same course of action will achieve different results at different times, he concludes that those who suit their own actions to "the times" succeed, while those who don't fail. Therefore, anyone who could "adapt to and understand the times ... could control the stars and the Fates" (*L. 121*).

This ideal flexibility is particularly recommended to princes. In *The Prince*, "the way to be absolutely successful in the contingent realm of human affairs is to be as flexible and capable of change as Fortune herself."[8] At the ideological heart of the work, where he claims to be stating the essential doctrine of ruling states, Machiavelli sums up the substance of the "rules" he has been laying down for the prince. If his ideal reader adopts these rules, "when fortune changes, it will find him in a position to resist" (*Pr. 14*). The nature of this resistance is made clear a few chapters later when Machiavelli explains that a successful ruler must "have a mind ready to shift as the winds of fortune ... may dictate," even if those winds demand that he perpetrate "evil" (*Pr. 18*). In effect, this princely advice encapsulates the ideal state of mind Machiavelli is recommending. Not by transcending fortune through heroic moral efforts—such as only the earliest, uncorrupted Romans could hope to do—but by internalizing her infinite variability may one attain the status of a true prince and adapt oneself to her every whim.

Unfortunately, this ideal posture exceeds human capability. Indeed, Machiavelli's "humanistic rationalism" leads him to emphasize "the inherent weaknesses of human nature," especially men's "lack of foresight and their inability to control their own nature."[9] In the final substantive chapter of *The Prince*, while noting that a prince who relies on fortune comes to grief as soon as she changes, Machiavelli is forced to retreat into the conditional: if such a man "*could* only change his nature with times and circumstances, his fortune would not change" (*Pr.* 25, my emphasis). If it is futile to expect to be able to shift with fortune's winds, it is equally "unreasonable ... to desire a change of fortune" (*Disc.* 2.23). Here we may suspect Machiavelli of secretly longing to transcend reliance on fortune. In a perfect state, citizens would be schooled to adapt themselves to the government they have, foregoing all desire for change.

The truth is that no one can always conform to fortune's changes. In reflecting on the nature and consequences of human ambition, Machiavelli notes that while all things fall within the scope of our desire, we always desire more than we can attain; hence the fluctuations of men's fortunes. In the *Ghiribizzi*, he elaborates: Anyone wise enough to adapt at all times would always have good fortune; but since such wise men do not exist, fortune controls men's outcomes. The reason for this inevitable shortfall lies in the gap between human desires and capacities. Because of this disconnect, our fortunes alter when fortune causes our circumstances to change but we cannot change our ways. Why is this so? Machiavelli spells out his answer in *Fortune*. One who was able to "jump from wheel to wheel" could be "content," but "this power is denied to us / By some mysterious force that governs us." Hence, "[w]ith the turn of the wheel our state must change." This explanation falls decidedly in the realm of the mystical. It is precisely a "hidden virtue" of the heavens—fortune's *virtù* as it were—that denies us the freedom to adapt to her vicissitudes.

On balance, then, Machiavelli recommends that we be wary of fortune's gifts. Perhaps the simplest formulation is that "*fortuna* is just one's situation." The "landscape" of *The Prince*'s dedication initiates a series of vignettes in the text that yields a new "prospect" demanding new "forms of action."[10] If one had to define this position, one might say that the individual should be skeptical of what may be on offer, yet ready at all times to benefit from any opening in her "warp" that may occur. This equivocal—perhaps even inconsistent—stance ranges from seizing the occasion, to adapting oneself to the times, to turning one's face to fortune. Difficult as these options may be to reconcile within a single coherent ideology, they do seem to share at least a modicum of human freedom, as well as a healthy skepticism regarding its limits.

Though all of these postures imply a fairly pessimistic outlook, the idea of seizing the occasion provided by fortune is closest to that of shifting with her changes. Here Machiavelli seems to be suspended between viewing fortune as a secret collaborator with the heroic individual and suspecting her at best of looking the other way while he seeks a way to evade her power. Not surprisingly, the more optimistic reading is deployed with respect to the ancients. Discussing the virtues of such founders as Moses, Cyrus, Romulus, and Theseus, Machiavelli boasts that "fortune provided nothing for them but the opportunity." At the end of the chapter, Machiavelli repeats the formula for that model opportunist, Hiero of Syracuse, who "owed nothing to fortune except the opportunity" (*Pr.* 6). The formula creeps in at minor junctures as well, as when Machiavelli justifies his unflattering comparison of his own time with that of the ancients by inviting his young readers to turn from one to the other whenever fortune allows them to do so (*Disc.* 2.Pr).

A variation on the fortune/occasion formula is adapting oneself to the times or to "circumstances." Once again, the difference between this prescription and shifting with fortune's changes is mainly the underlying assumption about men's freedom to circumvent her rule. The notion of adapting to the times is fully elaborated in the *Discourses*, especially 3.9, "That it behooves one to adapt Oneself to the Times if one wants to continue to enjoy Continued Good Fortune." In this discourse, Machiavelli openly wonders why men's fortunes vary and speculates that it is a function of their "conformity with the times." All men are inclined to make the mistakes dictated by their temperaments, but the individual is more likely to thrive when circumstances match his actions. Thus, Fabius Maximus prevailed because his circumspect behavior "fitted the circumstances." Implicitly, if the circumstances had altered, his behavior would have met with different results (*Disc.* 3.9). This conjecture becomes explicit with regard to Pope Julius, who thrived in his boldness, but would have failed "if circumstances had ever required him to act cautiously" (*Pr.* 25).

It is under the latter circumstances that Machiavelli invokes what is perhaps his most resonant formula for adapting to the reality of one's situation: turning one's face to fortune. It's difficult to capture the precise innuendoes of this often-repeated phrase. For example, in Francesco Sforza's rise to power in Milan, the then-count resolves to "show his face to fortune and to take counsel with its accidents." Endorsing this bravado, Machiavelli adds that such resolute action frequently reveals otherwise hidden "plans," implying that even when fortune's intentions are most obscure, the heroic response is to turn one's face to her, thus challenging her to disclose her well-kept secrets (*F.H.* 6.13).

Machiavelli is not averse to assuming such heroic bravado himself or recommending it to his friends. In an important letter to Francesco Vettori written shortly after his emergence from his ordeal at the time of the Medici restoration, Machiavelli responds to his friend's advice to turn his face to fortune. Citing this counsel in his reply, he boasts that he has borne the burden of his "troubles" like a man. Here, far from viewing fortune as a friend offering occasions to be seized, he adopts a stance of heroic defiance. In a lighter mood, responding to Vettori's account of a complex sexual adventure, he tries to bolster his friend's commitment to submit to Eros, advising him to "face Fortune squarely" and court the girl of his choice (*L.* 229). Though the erotic occasion may generate unintended results, Machiavelli, his tongue palpably in his cheek, urges the beleaguered Vettori to turn his face to fortune and brave the consequences. Despite the difference in tone, the trope strikes him as being as apt for the love-lorn Vettori as for the ambitious Sforza or himself at the nadir of his fortunes.

A number of disparate observations flesh out Machiavelli's view of fortune's workings. Perhaps the most fundamental is the basic need for plain good luck. This may be viewed as simply a weak, unanthropomorphized version of the mythic figure with her proverbial wheel. In speaking of the early history of Rome, he comments on "how extremely fortunate" she was to have first a belligerent king, then a pious and peaceful one, and then another warrior (*Disc.* 1.19). This good luck is repeated in modern times. After making the mistake of entrusting his fate to the "foreigner" Louis XII, it was "solely by his good luck" that Pope Julius was able to escape capture by his enemies (*Pr.* 13). Machiavelli's most contorted explication of the importance of luck comes at the beginning of his discourse on skirmishes. Since in all human affairs some evil is inextricably bound up with the good, to attain the latter requires luck: you must be "so aided by fortune that fortune itself eliminates this … inconvenience" (*Disc.* 3.37). In short, if you are lucky, luck will be on your side.

If the action of luck is as obscure as this statement implies, it is no surprise that its function is often linked with, or offered as an alternative to, other qualities. To overcome the difficulties inherent in acquiring new territories, for instance, "one needs good luck and plenty of resolution" (*Pr.* 3). In general, waging war requires good soldiers, wise generals, and good luck. Even for those who acquire states by virtue of the good luck of others, the latter must be accompanied by "good will" (*Pr.* 7). As always, of course, the alternative to trusting to luck—whether one's own or others'—is to rely only or mainly on one's own virtue. The two ways of becoming a prince, "by strength or by luck," are illustrated respectively by Francesco Sforza and Cesare Borgia. Whereas Sforza rose from private citizen to Duke of Milan by exercising his virtue, Duke Valentino gained and later lost power through the fortune of his father, the Pope. Despite his undoubted virtue, his vulnerability to fortune in the form of his father's untimely death makes him a paradigm of the vicissitudes of luck even to one who acts virtuously. If bad luck can be as powerful an agent of men's fates as good, it can be fended off by superior qualities. An army that is capable of withstanding multiple attacks in a single battle can be defeated only when thwarted by luck.

A stronger variation on good or bad luck entails the diverse "gifts" of fortune. These are rarely depicted as wholly arbitrary, but require at the very least a readiness on the part of their recipients to make use of them. Regarding Rome, Machiavelli observes that if it "did not get Fortune's first gift" of a primal lawgiver like Lycurgus, "it got its second" by establishing institutions on the right lines. Likewise, it was Rome's good fortune that fused Senate and plebs into a "perfect commonwealth" (*Disc.* 1.2). In bestowing her gifts, whether benign or malignant, fortune avails herself of men's virtues. When she wants a man to achieve greatness, she chooses one with the capacity and provides him the occasion to act; when she desires calamity, she chooses a different kind of agent; and when anyone opposes her will, she prevents his doing any good.

Machiavelli privileges the notion of fortune's favorites. Not only does he attribute an unusual degree of personality to fortune, but he often accords her a strong personal bias. Occasionally she is said to favor generic entities, such as the attacker over the defender. Normally, though, Machiavelli names specific groups—tribes, cities, nations—who have been favored by fortune. Rome, for one, was so favored that giving authority to the aristocracy didn't destroy the monarchy, nor did giving it to the populace abolish the aristocracy (*Disc.* 1.2). In modern times, Florence too has had her share of fortune's favors. During the period of her resistance to the Milanese under Francesco Sforza, divisions among the enemy commanders triggered an auspicious start to the hostilities because "fortune wanted to favor Florentine things" (*F.H.* 8.15). Similarly with individuals, when Spurius Postumius persuaded the Senate not to honor the peace treaty with the Samnites, "Fortune favored" him for the Samnites released him and he returned in "glory" (*Disc.* 3.42). Lorenzo de' Medici too "was loved by fortune and by God," as shown by his lucky escape from the Pazzi Conspiracy and other attempts on his life, his admiration by foreign rulers, and his other virtues (*F.H.* 8.6).

In preferring some men over others, fortune grants them specific favors. In the very first scene of *Mandragola*, Callimaco explains to his servant Siro that fortune brought Cammillo Calfucci to Paris in order to arouse his desire for Lucrezia. More portentously in *The Prince*, when fortune wants someone to rise to greatness, she gives him active enemies to overcome. In general, fortune finds a way to help her friends and hurt her enemies. Her interventions can take unexpected forms, turning her favorites' good fortunes to misfortunes. So in Machiavelli's semifictionalized biography, at the very moment when the Luccan army's defeat of the Florentines has brought Castruccio Castracani to the peak of his glory, a hostile fortune nudges him to expose himself to a cold wind, resulting in a fatal illness. *Sic gloria transit!*

How men respond when fortune bestows or withdraws her favors is as varied as the bestowal or withdrawal itself. Machiavelli cites two modern examples of great men trying to found cities who are unable to exploit their good fortune by killing those who bar their way. The first, Savonarola, simply lacked the "authority" to act as was required. The other, Piero Soderini, naively believed that his fortune would in time defeat envy; failing to realize that "fortune is changeable," he was doomed to lose power when envy inevitably brought him down (*Disc.* 3.30). Among the ancients, Machiavelli singles out the entire class of conspirators as men dependent on fortune. Thus Cataline and Hanno died in the attempt, whereas some Theban citizens succeeded by calling in a Spartan army. The best-laid plans of men go oft awry—or not, depending on whether or not they are favored by fortune.

This brings us to fortune's downside, misfortune, of which Machiavelli must have considered himself something of a connoisseur. By and large, misfortune is to be taken for granted as an inevitable, perhaps even normal, part of life. His friend Ercole Bentivoglio may be thought to speak *for* Machiavelli, as well as to him, when he writes of "our ill fortune in these times" (*L.* 107). Machiavelli speaks clearly enough for himself in "Fortune," when he depicts the blind goddess's indifference to men's hopes or merits. Fortune raises men to the height of prosperity, only to surrender them "to their foes as prey." Again, she lifts someone "to the spheres," not to keep him there but "to hurl him down" to her gleeful delight. Thus Cyrus and Pompey now lie "broken [and] dead," whom "yesterday / Fortune had taken to the sky." In light of this cold indifference to her victims, at his most pessimistic Machiavelli can take refuge in a mood of despair that negates the possibility of human agency. Even as he fulfills the obligation to acknowledge the deeds of others, he can't help but remind his reader that "the malignity ... of fortune" has prevented him from performing them himself (*Disc.* II.Pr).

Such despair at the prospects of misfortune is not Machiavelli's only, or even his usual, response. In less resentful moods he is happy to consider shifting the burden of responsibility to human agents. Thus the Florentine failure to take Lucca may have been due "either to mismanagement or to misfortune" (*Disc.* 1.8). He is even more insistent that defeat in battle has a human and not a metaphysical cause. A case in point is the wisdom of people when bad leadership has brought down disaster on them. Warning the leaders of a people's republic to avoid risky enterprises, he observes that when they are met with defeat the people blame not fortune but the general's ineptitude. Their response in such situations reflects the more rational side of Machiavelli himself, as opposed to the superstitious side that posits a malicious fortune bestowing her unwanted and undeserved gifts.

At times Machiavelli undertakes a rational analysis of misfortune that comports well with his more stoical view of human nature. On the basis of fortune's unpredictability, he subjects events to a search for causes. As always, the Romans provide the best case for such rational analysis. Because their fortune was inseparable from their virtue and prudence, it is easy to locate its cause. This analytical approach to fortune may even make it predictable. Thus when military units adapt similar formations, they suffer the same fortune. Yet the contrary condition vexes him. More than once he is led to ask why fortune awards "different results under similar circumstances" (*L.* 178). This is the query that prompts his meditation in the *Ghiribizzi* on the human incapacity to suit one's actions to the shifting winds of fortune. There, as we have seen, he comes to resign himself to the fact that no man is wise enough to rationalize fortune and enlist her on his side.[11]

Central to Machiavelli's speculations on human agency is the crucial relation of fortune to virtue. His persistent posing of this relation suggests that the pair of terms constitutes its own discrete arena of meaning. This is most obvious when he is formulating the existential conflict between human autonomy and the hostile or indifferent forces that seem to constrain it. But the conflict of virtue and fortune by no means exhausts their relationship. Perhaps even more frequently, Machiavelli posits a more neutral or even positive collaboration. The affirmation of this relationship can range from a habitual linking of the two—at times even a mere verbal tic—to exploring more complex connections between them.

Somewhat surprisingly, at times Machiavelli almost conceives virtue and fortune to be a single entity. Thus, in any calculation as to whether or not to initiate military action, a general stands to win or lose "according to his luck (*fortuna*) and to his virtue" (*Disc.* 2.22). Regarding Rome, he first asserts that the troubles resulting from the expulsion of the Tarquins were countered by her "good fortune," then adds that where military virtue obtains, good order and "good fortune" will follow (*Disc.* 1.4). The same inherent connection applies to individuals. When Charles VIII descended into Italy, he had already liberated his own country from the English "by his own virtue and good luck" (*Pr.* 13). In the final chapter of *The Prince*, he exhorts the Medici to lend the "fortune and ... virtue" of their house to the redemption of Italy (*Pr.* 26). Occasionally, though, he concedes that the two qualities don't always go together so neatly. Thus, he attributes Severus's peaceful death to his "great good luck and to his virtue, two things of which few men enjoy both" (*Disc.* 1.10).

The discontinuity of virtue and fortune is often conveyed by a simple variation on their formulaic coupling. When, for example, Machiavelli says that in the Romans' way of waging war virtue was "mingled with fortune," the verb implies that this mixture was by no means a common one (*Disc.* 2.1). Similarly, Livy's Romans rarely speak of "virtue without conjoining fortune" (*Disc.* 2.1). A different kind of conjunction/disjunction is invoked when one of these entities pertains to one party, the other to another, and they converge in yet a third. Such, according to Machiavelli, was the case among the descendants of the biblical King David. David left his son Solomon a stable realm in which to enjoy "the fruits of his father's virtue." Solomon's son Rehoboam, however, had trouble holding on to his inheritance because he lacked both his grandfather's virtue and his father's fortune (*Disc.* 1.19). Occasionally, this disjunction is broadened to imply some kind of causal relation. In founding Rome, for example, Aeneas's virtue is reflected in the city's fortune, an idea extended in the opinion that all rulers who possessed the same virtue would enjoy Rome's fortune. That men's virtues dispose fortune to grant them her favors is illustrated by Numa's establishing religion in early Rome, which fostered other institutions that in turn "led to good fortune" (*Disc.* 1.11). In the better days of the Florentine republic, Soderini's activities came to be viewed in the context of their accompanying good fortune. Machiavelli implies that in judging the conduct of an individual, people naturally infer the agent's virtue from his fortune.

Most often, Machiavelli conceives virtue and fortune in simple opposition. At its most basic level this opposition is conveyed in quasi-formulaic assertions of "virtue not fortune." For example, the great founders of civilizations like Moses, Cyrus, and the others prospered "by their own powers and not by accident" (*Pr.* 6). In the *Discourses*, Machiavelli reports the common belief that it was due to the

Romans' fortune, not their virtue, that they avoided getting embroiled in more than one war at a time. Whatever the case may have been with the Romans, in a modern state neither the prince nor his subjects can muster the virtue to prevail over fortune. Machiavelli insists that in general a state's autonomy depends on its arms. Without its own army a state "depends entirely on fortune" (*Pr.* 13). On occasion he rejects both options. Though ecclesiastical states are gained by either the one or the other quality, they can be held without either since they are buttressed by religion. Similarly, instead of by fortune or virtue, some private citizens rise to authority by either malfeasance or the choice of their fellow citizens.

Such an opposition of virtue and fortune can morph into their heroic disjunction. For example, in "Fortune" her power is said to rage on in great violence unless it is "checked by extreme *virtù*." On the other hand, where no such virtue manifests itself, fortune's sway is unlimited. This is what distinguishes modern from ancient republics. Whereas in the latter men and states take their fortunes into their own hands by exercising military virtue, in the former "where men have but little virtue, fortune makes a great display of its power" (*Disc.* 2.30). The sorry state of present-day Italy is elaborated near the end of *The Prince*, where fortune thrives in the absence of virtue. By contrast, as in the case of Agathocles, when virtue is present it leaves little room for fortune to flourish. Viewed in this disjunctive mode, the world offers men a stark choice between submitting to fortune or resisting her with their virtue.

Machiavelli's formulations can be more subtle. Such is his ironic allusion to the Venetians' explaining their good fortune by laying claim to a virtue they did not possess. In maintaining new states acquired "with Other People's Arms and by Good Luck," a prince must be ready to deploy his virtue in order to maintain fortune's gifts. If an individual is endowed with the requisite virtue, Machiavelli claims, he will quickly prepare himself to "preserve what fortune has showered on" him (*Pr.* 7). On the other hand, absent such virtue, fortune rapidly escapes men's control. After the Venetians' defeat by the French, they lost all of their territory because their lack of virtue left them despondent and therefore unable to rally. Had Venetian institutions had virtue, they could have easily resumed the struggle, either winning or losing with more honor and coming to better terms with their victors.[12] Lacking the virtue to either preserve or overcome fortune's power, men readily fall back into helplessness in her presence.

The inability to adapt to fortune's changes keeps men in her control. Viewed in light of the wide range of possible encounters of the self (or one's virtue) and fortune, this simplistic—even at times fatalistic—formula masks a stunning variety of potentialities. Given the frequency of Machiavelli's invocation of the virtue/fortune topos, it is hard to believe that this variety is due simply to chance verbalizations of an almost proverbial (or preverbal) nature. Perhaps we should concede that like the moon that conventionally symbolizes fortune's variability, Machiavelli's formulations reflect the changing moods in which he contemplates human freedom. Given the limitations of such abstract formulations, it may be that their contextualization in Machiavelli's literary works can help us to grasp these options more concretely. Two of his shorter poems offer a fairly stereotyped—one might say almost a poetic-paranoiac—version of the hostile goddess. In "Ambition" she is a remote and unfriendly power who strips us of happiness and vexes us with war. Most men fall readily into her hands, and one man weeps as he watches his fortune "snatched" by another. No one is spared her predations. Such scattered—and, on the whole, unreflecting—commonplaces evoke the late-Medieval figure familiar from hundreds of precursors.

In "Fortune," Machiavelli sharpens his focus on the powerful goddess. Here, if he does not completely transcend the usual stereotypes, he at least fleshes them out in great detail. Of all his capitoli on the major abstractions that define and shape our internal lives—ingratitude, fortune, ambition, and chance—this one is cast in the most heroic mould. The poem opens with the poet seeking inspiration to sing of "Fortune's sovereignty." At the end of the formal invocation, he challenges her to read his condemnation of her and concede that he "dares expose her, unafraid, alone." Having launched this challenge, the poem's speaker-singer proceeds to delineate her nature. All-powerful and two-faced, she rules from her high palace, which all can enter but none leave. Dominating an inconstant world, she revels in its inconstancy, desiring that nothing be eternal so we may more clearly discern her power. Given her absoluteness and the total irrationality of her nature, our only recourse is either to seize her when and as we can or adapt ourselves to her "whims."

The poem goes on to depict her actions, their effects, and the responses available to us. The essence of her behavior is its unpredictability. So pervasive is this feature that when she afflicts us she typically presents a world in metamorphosis. Seemingly accommodating, she shows her face to everyone, only to suddenly turn away and hide it. More than just unpredictable, she is quintessentially irrational, trampling down the just and exalting the unjust. Born with two faces, she arbitrarily picks winners and losers, but because she is treacherous, no one can count on remaining in her good graces. As an eagle smashes a turtle on a rock below and then dives down to feed on its flesh, so fortune raises her favorites up only to "hurl" them down and enjoy their misery. In general, she elicits curses from those within her sway, and the more they have been favored with wealth and power, the more quickly they express their "ingratitude," turning their backs on her former gifts. Among those who "lived happily" in the world, Alexander the Great and Julius Caesar are offered as extreme exemplars of "[h]ow much she loves and cherishes all those / Who push her, kick her, call her, and command her." Despite their fame and good fortune, Alexander fell short of the goal he most desired, and Caesar at the feet of the statue of his enemy Pompey. Of all those depicted in the scene, those fare best who adapt themselves to her "pace."

We have come full circle to Machiavelli's standard recommendation to adjust oneself to fortune. But the poem as a whole offers no such pragmatic counsel and ends on a bleak, uncompromising note. Just as elsewhere he had to concede that "no ... wise man exists," so here, after unfolding its survey of broken hopes and betrayed trust, the poem concludes that few men have ever been happy and that those who have were lucky enough to have died before their fortune changed. Only these men experienced "no ruinous fall." Machiavelli unrelentingly portrays fortune's realm as totally unresponsive to the human demand for justice. After the opening concession that our "virtue" may hold off her violence, the poem portrays her realm as harsh, alien, and irrational. While some men enjoy success in this life, such achievement is arbitrary, wholly unconnected with merit, and readily reversible. We are fundamentally slaves to fortune's whims, and only a timely death permits one to escape the turn of her wheel.

If we are to find in Machiavelli's literary works a less grim account of our freedom to escape her net, we must seek it in more dramatic, less abstract texts like the *Mandragola*.

Although the role of fortune is relatively muted in Machiavelli's great comedy, the very tentativeness of its deployment implies a subtler and perhaps deeper statement of that role than we have seen thus far. Insofar as its place in men's lives is explicitly addressed in the play, it is done so almost exclusively by the protagonist, Callimaco. But in order to properly appreciate this fact, we must first look at its implied function in the prologue. There, by dangling fortune before the reader-spectator as a potential scapegoat for his own thwarted virtue, Machiavelli prepares us to receive ironically his hapless protagonist's weak reliance on fortune and willingness to blame it for his own shortcomings.[13]

The prologue performs the hard work of audience disposition. In his own persona, after setting forth the play's story line and cast of characters, Machiavelli delivers a supposedly tongue-in-cheek apology for stooping to so low a genre. Acknowledging in advance his comedy's unworthy matter, he pleads as his excuse the fact that "he has nowhere else / to turn his face." The wording evokes Machiavelli's favorite bromide of turning one's face to fortune. The poignancy of his inability to do so prepares us for the claim that he has been "cut off" from all other outlets for displaying his virtue. It is in the context of the playwright-narrator's incapacity both to turn his face to fortune and to find an outlet for his virtue, that we must understand the dynamic in the play between its lover-protagonist, Callimaco, and its true "animator," Ligurio.[14]

From the outset, Callimaco defines himself as fortune's minion. When we first meet him, he attributes to fortune the sudden appearance in Paris of Cammillo Calfucci, whose description of his kinswoman Lucrezia inspires his return and her seduction. Callimaco's preoccupation with fortune becomes virtually an obsession in the soliloquy he delivers on the verge of success with Lucrezia. Although he invokes her by name only once—"It's true that fortune and nature hold the account in balance"—his entire posture in the scene is informed by the weakling's sense of reliance on forces beyond his control. The vocabulary is unmistakable: "What are you doing? Are you mad? ... Are you ashamed to go there? Face your lot; flee evil, but, not being able to flee it, bear it like a man; don't prostrate yourself, don't degrade yourself like a woman" (4.1).

Much as he reads his own life in terms of fortune's whims, he instinctively deploys its vocabulary with others. When he has prepared the potion that will ensure Nicia progeny, he informs him that "fortune has ... favored" him. Yet despite his being perfectly aware of the old man's denseness, even in soliloquy he couples meditations on his stupidity with the jealous concession that "fortune has favored him." Although the putative hero of the play, Callimaco's subscription to fortune, which illuminates his relative passivity in the hands of the virtuoso Ligurio, bears out the author's muting of fortune in his self-presentation in the prologue and allows us to appreciate the cunning of the play's chief moral agent.[15]

The other literary text relevant to this discussion, the unfinished *L'Asino*, is suffused with a sense of fortune's influence. From the outset, the narrator's Dantean journey is portrayed as a struggle to overcome a menacing fate, and throughout the poem he displays a sense of impending doom, which its opening lines announce he will have to overcome if he is to complete his "song." Even his metamorphosis is foreshadowed as a pushing back against a hostile universe. If "heaven overbrims with sneers/ Against me," he proclaims, "my loud bray" will pay them back with equal hurt. In a sense, the entire poem can be read as a transformation of fortune from a hostile to at least an indifferent adversary, if not a disguised friend, to individual agents.

The protagonist's education in the nature of fortune takes place at the hands of the beautiful handmaid of Circe, who conducts his philosophical-erotic education. While impressing on our hero the need for stoic indifference, a willingness to turn one's face to fortune, the lady promises that she will turn again in his favor if he only cultivates the proper posture. All of this is presented plausibly enough; yet the hint of a self-delusive stoicism is never completely absent from the text. When this attitude of stoic detachment metamorphoses into a closely related epicureanism in the person of the indulgent if philosophical pig, the satirical dimension of the odyssey resurfaces—to be left unresolved in the fragmentary poem.

The lady's tuition is designed to imbue the narrator with a proper disdain for fortune. Playing to his sense of victimhood—in ancient or modern times, she assures him, no one has ever endured such ingratitude as he—she concedes that it is his "ill luck" that has caused him such suffering. Nevertheless, he must manfully confront the blows of his fate. "Heaven," she continues, has not changed its opposition to him, nor will it until "the fates" relent. In the meantime, he must endure his fate until the heavens show themselves to be benign, at which time he will find happiness even in the recollection of his present sorrows. The narrator emerges from the lady's instruction grudgingly resigned. Refusing to lament his fate, he resolves to undertake the journey, defying "Fortune" to do her worst as she always has. His new resolve is buttressed by the feast the lady serves him as prelude to their lovemaking. Offering him wine, she proposes that they seize the day and accept that things fall as they must. Present misfortune will in time give way to good; the important thing is to make fortune your friend by embracing misfortune. Their reveling itself furnishes the metaphor for her doctrine: the trick is "when misfortune strikes," to "gulp it down like medicine"—and so they do, happily feasting before falling into bed. Whatever the persuasive powers of the lady's erotic charms, the narrator emerges from their tryst imbued with her philosophy.

After she departs in the morning to fulfill "the will of fortune," he is somewhat mysteriously moved to reflect on the fate of nations.[16] The theme of his meditation echoes her instruction. Contemplating the ebb and flow of large historical events, he comes to see them as part of a universal scheme. Though the tide may at any time turn against us, giving us the impression of a hostile universe, if we grasp the ultimate order of human affairs we will maintain control of ourselves, if not of these external forces. In this way we ultimately become active partners in the fulfillment of heaven's will, in short, agents of change. The apprehension of this universal scheme proposed by the lady and internalized by the narrator is subject to considerable ironic stress when the pig launches into a passionate repudiation of the human condition, doomed he says first by "nature" then by "fortune," and cheerfully renounces the miseries generated by men's ambition, lust, and greed, while affirming his own happiness as superior to any specious version claimed by some allegedly "divine man."

With this implicit, and we suspect ironic, fatalism, we take leave of Machiavelli's literary forays into the realm of fortune. The epicurean pig is hardly a convincing alternative, let alone a potent antidote, to any of Machiavelli's philosophizing personae, including the stoical lady in the same poem. And we have no clue as to how he would have extracted himself from what strikes us in the poem we have as a philosophical and moral *cul-de-sac*. Is the indulgent pig Machiavelli's final incarnation of his recommended indifference to "nature and fortune," the ultimate manifestation of an attitude emerging from the narrator's own ruminations as supported by the lady's instruction? Or is it a *reductio ad absurdum* of that philosophical drift? Given its satirical presentation, we might be tempted to opt for the latter. But Machiavelli, as the tantalizing smile in his portraits reminds us, is an audacious and unpredictable writer, not easily reduced to the usual critical canons.[17] And just as *L'Asino* itself ends abruptly with the pig's assertion of his mindless contentment in the mud, so its author is content to revel in the blank image of animal hedonism with which his poem ends. For better or worse, from *this* world both fortune and our itch to comprehend her have been definitively banned.

CHAPTER 6

MACHIAVELLI THE WRITER

In taking up the question of Machiavelli's literary stature, we once again face the odd bifurcation at the heart of our subject. The Machiavelli of tradition, fixed in the collective consciousness by the pejorative epithet "Machiavellian," is the master political theorist of *The Prince.* Even if this persona is not (mis)taken for a "teacher of evil," at the very least he is an objective observer of the political scene, whose austere pronouncements leave little room for the kind of imaginative play we normally associate with creative writing. We might label this figure the "prosaic" Machiavelli, except that even as a writer of prose Machiavelli did not limit himself to this posture. It may surprise some readers to learn that in his own lifetime Machiavelli's fame was based almost entirely on his dramatic writings, especially the *Mandragola;* only after his death did the focus shift to the moral content of his thought.[1]

To reduce Machiavelli's purely literary production to a mere footnote to his musings on matters of state, therefore, would misrepresent its place in his life. Especially after the end of his active participation in republican government, writing became the essence of Machiavelli's life. He did a lot of it, took it seriously, and saw it—as he saw virtually everything he did—as part and parcel of the active life of a citizen, whether in a functioning republic or in a principality. It is this quintessentially Machiavellian engagement that I wish to foreground in the following discussion. Even among his miscellaneous lyrics we find poems embedded in the poet's political life, like the "prison sonnets" to Giuliano de' Medici, the *capitoli* ("chapters") on the fate of grand human aspirations, the biting epigram on Piero Soderini, and the meditations on fortune and the state of Europe in *L'Asino*. In the last of these especially, we are able to sense Machiavelli's effort to appropriate his beloved Dante in the service of a personal odyssey that never seriously tries to transcend the political. This is even more the case with the greatest of his comedies, the *Mandragola*, in which he tries to convey the complex relations between the exiled writer and his city.

Before surveying Machiavelli's *oeuvre*, we might look briefly at his self-definition as a writer. Early in his writing life, Machiavelli seems to have viewed himself principally as a poet. This claim is made explicitly in two "sonnets" addressed to Giuliano de' Medici shortly after the poet's release from prison. In the first, Machiavelli begins by linking his ordeal in the Medici prison with his status as a poet: "thus are treated those who deal with rhymes." In the sequel, mistaken by one of the Muses for a contemporary scribbler because of his abject condition, he begs his patron to testify that he is indeed himself. When, near the end of the first edition of his comic epic masterpiece *Orlando furioso*, Ariosto excludes Machiavelli from the group of (mostly mediocre) poets that salutes his triumph, the latter complained of being omitted "like some prick" (L. 254, December 17, 1517).[2]

Elsewhere, Machiavelli burnishes his literary image. At the end of a letter written to Guicciardini, he famously signs himself "Niccolò Machiavelli, *istorico, comico e tragico*" (L. 300, after October 21, 1525), proudly suggesting the breadth of his literary output. Perhaps his fullest, and certainly his most ironic, self-portrait as a writer comes in the prologue to the *Mandragola*, where writing is associated with his fall "from ancient virtue." If writing in the literary sense constitutes an unworthy occupation for "a man who wishes to seem wise and grave," his sole excuse is that lacking any more profitable alternative he is "trying / with these vain thoughts / to make his wretched time more pleasant." Overall, his reflections on the enforced vocation of his later years oscillated between self-scorn and self-vindication.

As a writer, Machiavelli was prolific. After a modest output of lyric poems in his earlier years, he wrote *The Prince* shortly after his fall in 1513. By that time he had already begun the *Discourses*, whose composition he interrupted to write the shorter treatise. He must have completed them within a few years, for he dedicated the *Discourses* to two of the free-thinking young aristocrats who frequented the Orti Oricellari around 1514–1515. He also assigned *The Art of War*, which is set there, the fictive date of 1516. In the same period, he wrote the fragmentary *L'Asino*, probably his novella *Belfagor*, and, if he was indeed its author, the *Dialogue Concerning Our Language*; translated Terence's *Andria*; and began his masterpiece, the *Mandragola*, which was completed by 1518. The *Florentine Histories* were commissioned in 1520, also the most likely date of the *Life of Castruccio Castracani*. His second comedy, the *Clizia*, was first produced in January 1525. In addition, he produced prose works in various genres. Putting aside his personal letters, the dispatches alone fill several volumes. Besides the works already mentioned, he authored tracts and treatises too numerous to discuss here that were of immediate import to his city.[3]

L'Asino aside, Machiavelli's poems fall into categories ranging from those consisting of several hundred lines to the pithiest of lyrics. Of the former, his major production is the serenade "Salve, donna." Composed in ottava rima, or what English readers like to call the "*Don Juan* stanza" (abababcc), the poem is a long appeal to the speaker's coy mistress in which he invokes Pomona, from Ovid's *Metamorphoses* to warn against the vengeance of an "irate" Venus. The twist is that her lover Vertumnus is also a narrator, who courts *his* recalcitrant maid by telling her the story of Iphis and Anaxarete. Failing to break through her defenses, the hapless lover hangs himself at Anaxarete's door. At his funeral, the repentant lady is suddenly transformed to stone, an outward manifestation of her inner hardness. Profiting from Anaxarete's example, Pomona yields to her lover and enjoys a lifetime of "bliss"; the speaker urges his lady to do the same.

Machiavelli's three major capitoli are poetic meditations on moral abstractions. Each is dedicated to an individual of Machiavelli's acquaintance and purports to instruct the addressee drawing on the speaker's own experience. In "Ingratitude," Machiavelli addresses his friend Giovanni Folchi, whose involvement in the Boscoli conspiracy in 1510 may have led to Machiavelli's own brief imprisonment and torture. Here the speaker bemoans his own suffering from the ingratitude of others, buttressing his personal experience with forays into conventional allegory and abstract pronouncements on its worldly ambiance. The core of the poem depicts ingratitude's main historical victims: Scipio, Themistocles, and Caesar among the ancients; Achmet Pasha and Gonzalvo Fernandez de Cordova among the moderns. "Ingratitude" ends with a typically Machiavellian blast at the ingratitude awarded "those who free a state" or give up their princedoms, conventionally urging his reader to "abhor both court and state."

Dedicated to Giovanni Battista Soderini, Piero's nephew, "Fortune" too stakes out a position of moral detachment and superiority to those who succumb to her sway. As we saw in Chapter 5, this two-faced deity incarnates the irrationality of the world and its indifference to the merits of those who seek power. Though there is the obligatory smattering of lesser allegorical figures—for example, Fear, Envy, Repentance, Necessity, Sloth, Patience, Usury, Fraud, Liberality, "Case" (= *Caso*, chance), and Luck—and of historical exemplars like Memphis, Thebes, and Babylon, the best parts of the poem delineate fortune's tragic consequences. Because, driven by our natures we are incapable of adjusting to what our intellects tell us is needed to succeed, we are left stranded, solitary and impotent to escape. As noted earlier, the poem ends by grimly posing the equally unsatisfying alternatives of suffering a downturn of fortune's wheel or dying before the inescapable "ruinous fall."[4]

The last of Machiavelli's major capitoli is "Ambition," dedicated to Francesco Guicciardini's eldest brother, Luigi. Here the speaker warns his naive addressee that wherever he roams in the world, Ambition and Greed will follow him. Nearly as old as man himself, these "two furies" were hurled down to deprive us of all serenity. The speaker bitterly reflects on the insatiable malignancy of men's minds and the wholesale suffering inflicted on ordinary men and women by ambitious princes. These ruminations are punctuated by historical examples such as the king of France and the "fratricidal wounds" inflicted on Siena and Florence. The latter especially inspires fear that Tuscany will soon fall prey to ambition, and the poem ends by conjuring the prospect of neighboring territory utterly destroyed if her "sparks" are not doused by "grace or better order."

Generically related to these three capitoli, the slightly shorter "Pastoral Chapter" features a conventional shepherd who takes refuge in the shade of a laurel tree to move nature Orpheus-like with his song. The subject of his "hymn" is the Ovidian Hyacinthus, nature's gift to the ambient world, and its prayed-for effect lending comfort to grieving lovers. The burden of the poem is extravagant praise of the mythological hero blessed by Vulcan, Jove, Minerva, Venus, Mars, Mercury, Juno, and Saturn with their respective gifts of intellect, mercy, and beauty.

This generosity is appropriated by the lowly singer, who, transfigured and exalted by his subject, humbly dedicates his talents and his "flock" to Hyacinth. The poem ends conventionally with dusk's descent impelling the singer to seek repose till another day invites him to resume his praises.

Somewhat less expansive than the capitoli, Machiavelli's Carnival Songs provide an apt medium for their author's quizzical outlook on human, especially erotic, endeavors. His "Demons Thrown Out of Heaven" find on earth a scene ripe for their rule, with lovers especially worthy of their dubious gifts. In "Desperate Lovers and Ladies," two semi-choruses each blame the other for the pangs of love. Both subject and tone turn more somber in "The Blessed Spirits," where the titular singers bemoan the desolation wreaked on earth by warring nations and sects. Likewise, "The Hermits" descend to calm the city's fear of imminent "disasters," inviting the Carnival ladies to share their own serenity. Reverting to the love-theme, the somewhat bizarre "Pine-Cone Vendors" gently satirize the conduct of both sexes, but especially women, in the timeless love game. Finally, in the same spirit, the transparently phallic "Snake Charmers" dangle the "harms" and "remedies" that promise the ladies "heavenly ... bliss."

Machiavelli's shorter poems exhibit a similar range of subjects and tones. Dedicated to Filippo de' Neri, "Chance" features a dialogue between an anonymous prompter and the eponymous heroine, who defines herself and her companion Penance. Other short forms utilized by Machiavelli include the sonnet, the strambotto, and the epigram.[5] His sonnets vary in form, the only "regular" (14-line) exemplar being the conventional complaint, "If for one hour I could not think of you." The elongated sonnet "To Messer Bernardo, His Father" conveys a realistic report on his own situation in Florence. Even less conventional are the three "Prison Sonnets" directed to Giuliano, son of Lorenzo the Magnificent. As we have seen, the first portrays Machiavelli's situation following his ordeal of six drops, while the next describes the visit of his Muse. In the last he accompanies the gift of some thrushes with a light allegory of men's habit of feeding on their own flesh.

In addition to his sonnets, Machiavelli has a number of short poems in various meters. The conventionality of their forms is belied by the occasional twist they take, generally toward the topical and the mundane. His 24-line "Song:" "If you had wings and bow," flatters an anonymous "lad of glee"—the Italian *giulío* suggests that the poem is addressed to Giuliano, the son of Lorenzo il Magnifico—with a comparison to Jupiter's beloved Ganymede. Two other lyrics are dedicated to Machiavelli's beloved, Barbara Raffacani Salutati. The first, "At the Request of Barbera," is a dual celebration of the speaker's lady and Eros, concluding that the latter "I shall call my lord, and you, my God." In the even terser "To Barbera," the speaker blames not Love but himself for loving a "beauty" that perforce seeks pleasure in a "greener age."

Concluding this inventory of Machiavelli's shorter poems are his strambotti and epigrams. The strambotto "I hope, and oh, to hope is to ache more" plays riffs on the conventional Petrarchan oxymora of the despairing lover: "I weep … I laugh … I burn." In "Each beast conceals the arms of his attacks" a menagerie of creatures emblematize the injuries inflicted by the heartless lady. Of his epigrams the better known is that on the death of the poet's former boss, the gonfalonier in the 1494–1512 Florentine Republic. "The night Pier Soderini passed away," the poet tells us, Pluto denied him entrance to Hell, redirecting him instead to "limbo among the other children." In "I am not Argus," we see an example of Machiavelli's idiosyncratic appropriation of a popular motif. Here the speaker, who may or may not be the conventional jealous lover, boasts that he has stolen his (hundred?) eyes from "Christian princes," whose blindness has led the mad Charles V and the Viceroy of Naples, Charles de Lannoy, to abandon the king of France, François I.

Machiavelli's sole work of prose fiction, the nine-page satirical novella *Belfagor*, vindicates its author's contemporary reputation as a storyteller. The narrative is relatively straightforward. Repeated complaints by the damned compel Pluto to order an examination of the institution of marriage. In Council the devils resolve to settle the issue by selecting one of their number to take a wife. The lot falls to Belfagor, who, abundantly funded, descends to Florence and marries a girl named Onesta, with whom he promptly falls in love. His doting affection for his wife soon fans her pride, which she indulges to his great cost. Eventually bankrupt by her extravagances, he flees, taking refuge with a farmer, Gianmatteo del Brica, with whom he sets up a lucrative charade of expelling devils, always of course himself. Belfagor has just announced to his host that the game is over when the farmer is ordered to "cure" the daughter of the French king, Louis VII. Belfagor has planned this possession as a way to get even with the now-wealthy Gianmatteo, who is threatened with hanging if he fails to cure the princess. Thus cornered, he scares the devil into expelling himself by staging the noisy approach of his wife, a prospect that drives him to abandon the world and take refuge in the relative serenity of Hell.

However slight its conceit, Machiavelli's novella displays his narrative gifts. We have already met the basic premise of a devil set at large in the human world in one of the Carnival Songs. This situation is exploited with the stock motif of a shrewd peasant's sparring with the Devil. The story conveys Machiavelli's assault on women, triggered by sinners' reports that marriage has landed them in Hell. Its crux is Onesta's self-indulgent response to her husband's affection, the mental and financial burden effects of her pride generating the sardonic force of the tale's denouement. At the crucial moment when the recalcitrant devil refuses to be expelled from the princess's body, the shrewd peasant knows exactly how to conjure him, the mere word *wife* acting as a potent emetic. In the end, the misogynistic theme fuses seamlessly with the motifs of devils-in-the-world and the peasant who outwits the Devil.

Machiavelli's skill in fusing these diverse elements vindicates *Belfagor*'s critical status. The story shows how he earned his reputation as a great storyteller, for which we must otherwise rely on his racier letters. The vividness of detail, especially in imagining the minutiae of quotidian life through the sensibility of an alien infernal invader, underscores the sense of reality, particularly Florentine reality that we associate with Machiavelli. Brief and conventional as it is, *Belfagor* succeeds because it is unmistakably situated in the Florence of his time. If that is no compliment to his native city, we could expect no more from the man who prides himself on the art of "speaking ill."

These literary skills are nowhere more evident than in his vivid and often raucous personal letters, which establish Machiavelli as "a prince, a molder and founder of principalities through the imaginative exercise of his comic art."[6] In both specifics and atmospherics, his most famous letter is also a sterling example. Reciprocating his friend Vettori's account of his days in Rome, Machiavelli tells how, after inspecting his woods and "slum[ming] around" with the townsfolk at an inn, he returns home to don his court clothes and "step inside the venerable courts of the ancients." From these gleanings he has put together a "whimsy," *The Prince*, that should please his friend (L. 224, December 10, 1513). More than anything else, it's the strong verbs that bring to life this snapshot of the banality of involuntary retirement. Six months later he will famously describe his existence as "rotting away … amid my lice" (L. 236, June 10, 1514), but the earlier account conjures up a much more self-assertive and self-transforming persona.

I will return to Machiavelli's self-transformations in a moment, but first two other letters may serve to illustrate his narrative and descriptive powers. In 1521, Machiavelli found himself at Carpi, a small town west of Ferrara, seeking a preacher for Florence. From there he writes his new friend Guicciardini while sitting on the toilet and contemplating "the absurdities of this world," imagining ways of provoking the assessors so they'll start "going after one another with their wooden clogs," and relating how he had dazzled the gaping friars with stories of his secret dispatches about the emperor, the Swiss, and so forth. (L. 270, May 17, 1521). Even more graphic is Machiavelli's famous account to Guicciardini of his encounter with an old whore during his stay in Verona. There, invited by an old woman into her house to look at some shirts, he found another woman cowering in the shadows. He had sex with her, only to discover afterwards that she was so disgustingly ugly that he threw up, resolving never to "get horny again" (L. 178, December 8, 1509). In both of these examples, Machiavelli himself is the main focus, in the one case as wily manipulator, and in the other as innocent victim.[7]

Other letters about love-trysts display Machiavelli's lighter, more playful side. This may be partly explained by the subject, partly by the fact that the follies described are not his own but those of his friends. Vettori had written Machiavelli of a pleasant evening spent with his neighbor and her children, when the girl, whom Vettori himself fancied, had been courted by Giuliano Brancacci and the boy by Filippo Casavecchia. A few weeks later, Machiavelli playfully recreates the scene, to which Vettori replies by continuing the story of Costanza, to whom he has offered himself "as prey" (L. 230, February 9, 1514). In the same spirit, Machiavelli now regales his friend with a delightful "yarn" centering on a "laughable metamorphosis." Failing to find any birds in a wood in Rome, he lands a young thrush at the goldsmith's, where "he minister[s] to several of its hind feathers" and puts it in his pouch. Brancacci finds out who the boy is, tells him that he himself is Casavecchia, and invites him to his shop, where the real Casavecchia proceeds to unravel the trick. Casavecchia is exonerated, Brancacci exposed, and all through the carnival season Rome echoes with the chant, "Are you Brancacci or are you Casa?" (L. 231, February 25, 1514). In this parable Machiavelli attains a personal pinnacle in the prose rendering of erotic fancy.[8]

Turning to Machiavelli's unfinished verse satire, *L'Asino*, it may be well to begin by stating what little we know about the poem's composition. Begun sometime before 1517, it was abandoned not long thereafter. The reason Machiavelli gave up on the text is unclear, but he may have done so after reading the manuscript of Ariosto's *Orlando furioso* not long after its publication in 1516. Possibly concluding that he could not compete with the master in this genre, he turned to comedy, first translating Terence's *Andria*, and then composing his masterpiece, the *Mandragola*. Technically, *L'Asino* is akin to Machiavelli's capitoli. Not only does it share the latter's meter, terza rima, but each of its chapters is roughly the length of the three major capitoli discussed previously, 120–150 lines or fewer. And though it remains a fragment, enough was completed to give us a good idea of its scope and intention.[9]

The shape of the poem can be worked out on the basis of the completed portion and the hints Machiavelli gives us in its opening lines. While the narrator's metamorphosis never occurs in the text as we have it, Chapter 1 begins by alluding to the "ass's skin I had to bear" and ends by warning his reader to beware this "beast" and his "asinine . . . jokes." It's by no means clear when this transformation would have taken place. Unlike his prototype, the narrator has his amatory adventure in human, not asinine, form, and he is still unmetamorphosed when he undertakes his odyssey among the other animals. The descent into "asininity" may be Machiavelli's way of "turning his face to fortune," the mark of the Machiavellian wise man who knows when to resign himself to his circumstances and when to oppose them by "speaking ill." Likewise, by turning to satire Machiavelli responds to the misfortunes attendant on his exile and the rejection or failure of his literary gifts.[10]

Both the choice of terza rima and the contours of the protagonist's quest underscore the strong Dantean provenance of the tale. The generic romance opening of the narrative in Chapter 2, "When the bright spring returns ... ," soon gives way to a specific Dantean echo, when the narrator suddenly finds himself in a dark wooded dale. The Machiavellian appropriation of Dante peaks when the narrator, like Dante with Beatrice in the Earthly Paradise, is too mortified to explain his fall to the lady. Echo becomes parody in Chapter 3, when the Donna reveals his fortune to him, ascribing his innocent sufferings to a malignant instability of things. All memory of Dante fades as the narrative merges prophecy with erotic indulgence.

On the other hand, in his treatment of the narrator Machiavelli departs from his Dantean model. In Chapter 1, Machiavelli portrays his asinine persona as driven by an insuppressible need to divulge the defects of others. He underscores the motif by rehearsing the story of a young Florentine who feels compelled to run whenever he sees an alluring roadway. Despite a physician's "cure," the sight of the Largo sparks the young man's imagination and he returns to his obsession. In the same way the times draw the narrator inexorably back to *his* old, ingrained habit of indulging in his own "asinine jokes." Within the narrative proper, however, this wildness is replaced by the timidity of the speechless voyager rescued by the lady in Chapter 2. Despite his festive revival in the intervening chapters, in Chapter 4 he is still the fading violet cowering in his blanket like a bride wrapped in her sheets. Chastised by his hostess for his small courage, he embraces her and agrees to adopt the role of the Dantean voyager-reporter.

Initially *L'Asino* falls into several discrete "essays," each displaying its unique thematic emphasis. For example, the first chapter presents the signature Machiavellian proposition of an irreversible bias that defines the individual. Asserting "an ass's bray" as his muse and music, the speaker promises that it will resound to its hearers' discomfort. Couched in the language of natural habit, the story of the young Florentine runner underscores the speaker's own obsessive verbal habits. He too has tried "another way" but can't shake his habit of speaking ill. Similarly tainted with an asinine compulsion to run, Machiavelli's persona is compelled to bray by material provided by "[o]ur present time."

In the second chapter, the emphasis is on the speaker's reenactment of Dante's providential redemption in the dark wood. Machiavelli telescopes Vergil and Beatrice into the figure of Circe's handmaid. After its conventional romance opening, amidst the roaring of "small donkeys," the speaker finds himself just before dawn in a grisly place, suddenly deprived of his "soul's freedom." Terrified by the loud sound of a horn and seeming to spy Death with his scythe, he at last sees the approach of the lady, carrying a horn and a lantern and accompanied by various beasts, who follow her hand in hand. Like the scene itself, his rescuer has some sharp edges, greeting him twice "with a leer" before explaining who she is and compelling him to follow her home, creeping among the other animals.

Virtually half of Chapter 3 is taken up with the voyager's account of his apprehension as he crawls into her bedroom and with his apology for his previous silence. When he finally summons up the courage to ask her about his future, her response is grim but bracing. No one, she assures him, ancient or modern, has suffered "Ingratitude's foul crimes" as he has done. Yet being a man, he must face his fate dry-eyed. Focusing his mind on the inexorable variability of the natural order, she reminds him that in due course his fortunes will change; in the mean time, for his own benefit fate has determined that he "must observe the world ... beneath a different skin." Encouraging him to shoulder his burden, she promises that one day he will be grateful for the chance. If the lady's prophecy stresses the arduousness of the speaker's ordeal and the courage required to endure it, the love-tryst in Chapter 4 couches his fate in a riot of sensuality. The perfunctory feast dispensed with, she quickly undresses her lover and leads him to bed. Here the scene turns comical, as the speaker's timidity prompts her to urge him to take the plunge.

In contrast to the sharply focused scenes just rehearsed, the second half of the poem is more expansive and therefore less compelling. Following the speaker's meditation on the fate of nations in Chapter 5, the lady, and even the speaker himself, become secondary to the allegory that is imperfectly conducted in Chapter 8. To some extent the pig's monologue reinforces the narrator's own reflections in Chapter 5 on the appetite for fame and material goods that drives men. Here chapter and poem end, with both traveler and reader left to ponder whether all human striving for excellence are reduced to a perversion of nature. Whether this was the poem's intended culmination, we will never know. As it stands, for all its allusions to the narrator's "braying" at his audience, the conflict between speaker and world is hardly engaged in the text and the threat of lacerating his reader with ill speech never really comes off. The place where it was most likely to have occurred, the Dantean report of his descent to the inferno of allegorical beasts, is both the most fragmentary and the least successfully articulated part of the poem. And the fact that it is capped by the pig's unanswered defense of a life of sensual indulgence leaves us uncertain as to the ultimate target of Machiavelli's satire.[11] Despite its local virtues, then, the ultimate effect of *L'Asino* is to direct us even more desperately to the comedies in order to define Machiavelli's literary impulse.

Machiavelli's first venture into comedy was his translation of Terence's *Andria*.[12] The event is less important as a literary phenomenon than as evidence that the author was steeped in the conventions of Roman New Comedy. The plot turns on the traditional struggle between paternal authority and filial rebellion. Panfilo's father, Simo, wants him to marry Cremete's daughter, Filomena, for her dowry, but Panfilo himself is in love with Glicerio. A fake wedding between Panfilo and Filomena, designed to smoke out Panfilo's intentions, is thwarted by Simo's wily slave Davo, who announces that Glicerio is pregnant. When in addition Carino reveals his love for Filomena to his friend Panfilo, they too conspire to block the wedding. Even when Davo reports that Cremete doesn't want Filomena to marry Panfilo, the latter agrees to marry Filomena, believing that Simo wants to blame Panfilo for the thwarted marriage. Cremete reluctantly agrees to the match, at which point Panfilo decides that only a new ploy can rescue him. Davo scares Cremete off by forcing Glicerio's maid, Miside, to announce Glicerio's baby as Panfilo's, adding the rumor that Glicerio is an Athenian and hence Panfilo will have to marry her. Supported by Cremete's newly arrived friend Crito, Simo throws in the towel, Panfilo agrees to follow Simo's will in everything so long as he concedes that Panfilo didn't bring Crito to Athens, and Crito reveals that the stranger is Cremete's brother. Therefore both Panfilo and Simo will get what they want, and Carino will have his Filomena.

This complicated synopsis makes clear Machiavelli's debt to classical comedy. The play achieves its comic resolution through the belated appearance of Crito. As opposed to the flexible Simo, the protean Davo, and his sometime disciple Panfilo, Crito authenticates the second "Andria," Glicerio—who ironically turns out to be authentic because she is *not* an Andria but an Athenian—on the basis of his credibility. The hero Panfilo is a similarly dependable character, whose identity rests on his unvarying devotion to Glicerio, but who puts all in jeopardy by following the counsel of Davo and un-saying that commitment. One ramification of Panfilo's choice is that no one in the play, not even Panfilo, can be reliably held to be what he or she seems, at least until the entrance of the honest Crito. Especially in its exposé of the slipperiness of reputations, the complexity and importance of their social contexts, and the risks involved in manipulating appearances to one's particular ends, the *Andria* anticipates Machiavelli's original comedies. In the always fragile machinations of the conventional Davo, we can foresee the more masterful plottings of Machiavelli's most original creation, Ligurio.

At first blush, the *Mandragola* appears to be a pristine Roman New Comedy. The basic ingredients are all there: the young lovers, the "blocking figure" of a *senex* or old man, and the wily slave or parasite paving the hero's way to the lady's bed. Only a rapacious friar and the girl's easy-going mother are needed to complete the list of *dramatis personae*. The play opens with the lover, Callimaco, a Florentine exile who has been living in Paris, rehearsing how he fell in love while hearing Lucrezia praised, much as his Livian prototype Tarquinius does with her namesake, Lucretia. To accomplish her seduction, he has engaged a factotum named Ligurio, who has persuaded Nicia, the lady's aging husband, that his lack of an heir is due to Lucretia's infertility. The doctor he has found to cure her turns out to be Callimaco and the proposed cure a draught of mandragola, the catch being that the first man to sleep with her after she takes it will die. The remedy is to "sacrifice" someone in a one-nighter, after which Nicia and Lucrezia may resume their now-fertile relations. The latter of course will be Callimaco in disguise.

This basic plot is spun with various delicious complications. A minor obstacle is the lady herself, who is chaste and pious, but here the remedy will be her confessor, the easily bribed Fra Timoteo. He, in turn, will be abetted by her mother, Sostrata, who wants a child for her daughter as much as do the lady and her husband. Ligurio pays the friar to help with the seduction, the "potion" is secured, and Callimaco is wrestled into her bed. In the morning, Callimaco rehearses the night's pleasures to Ligurio, including his promise to marry her when Nicia dies, as well as Nicia's offer of free access to their house in exchange for the promised heir. In the final scene, this promise is consecrated at the church door, where the party proceeds for a pregnancy blessing by the well-paid friar.

On the face of it, the play sticks closely to the boy-gets-girl formula. But from the outset, the intrigue is embedded in its political-historical context. In his exposition, Callimaco evokes the action's precise historical moment: born in Florence in 1474, he was sent to Paris in 1484, and has been settled there for ten years at the time of Charles VIII's invasion, 1494, the play's dramatic date, at which time he hears of Lucrezia's beauty and decides to return to Florence. Much of the comedy springs from the characterization of Nicia. At times little more than the conventional aging cuckold with a weakness for anyone who can sprinkle his speech with Latin, he is understandably (and sympathetically) reluctant to assist in his own cuckolding and at times is granted moments of real insight to offset his conventional stupidity. If in the end he comes across as the butt of most of the humor and intrigue, his driving motive, the desire to have an heir, is shared by his young wife and, to an extent, her mother. Indeed, there is something unsettling in making this nearly universal motive the hook for so much of the play's unrelieved folly and derision.[13]

As for Lucrezia, she is a shadowy victim of the male protagonists. By the time she first appears at the end of the third act, we have heard from Nicia about her earlier experience with lustful friars as well as her extreme piety. But her first speech in the play, addressed to her mother, reveals a sense of honor and a revulsion from sacrificing an innocent stranger in the process of losing it, while her passive role in the combined assault by Timoteo and Sostrata shows her departing from a familiar moral world taken on faith into an unknown one identified in her own mind with spiritual death. Her last words before her fall are a simple prayer to God and the Virgin to preserve her from harm; her next are those reported by Callimaco after their tryst, by which she adapts a newly discovered self to a new world under his protection. Here, in a mood of resignation to a moral universe not her own, she acknowledges that the combined forces of his "astuteness," Nicia's "stupidity," Sostrata's "simplicity," and Timoteo's "wickedness" have compelled her to do "what I never would have done by myself." From this improbable event she infers the workings of "a heavenly disposition" she lacks the power to resist.

Is the irony hers or Machiavelli's? Much has been made of Lucrezia's rebirth as a Machiavellian New Woman whose worldliness is born of a sexual initiation that liberates her own suppressed desires. But she herself confesses to no such transfiguring pleasure, either to Callimaco in his report or to the audience when she reappears in the following scene. Instead, we find a few swift traces of an assertive young wife who will probably exact a more painful price from her doddering husband than a mere cuckolding for the production of heirs. On balance it seems likely that the new Lucrezia is intended to appear no more self-created in her disillusionment than her prototype. She has simply adopted a new, and perhaps more gratifying, set of moral values from characters who command little of our respect and is conditioned to move in a world constructed and controlled by others. For this reason, perhaps, rather than as a result of her initiation into sexual pleasure, she anoints Callimaco as her "lord, master, and guide."[14]

As for the play's putative hero, Callimaco is something of a chameleon. He proves himself adept at picking up Ligurio's cue about the mandrake-root and running with it—unless he has been coached offstage. Callimaco is often viewed as a Machiavellian prince under the tutelage of his adviser Ligurio, whose metamorphoses—into first a doctor, and then the unfortunate "lout"—are imposed by a mimetic or derived desire for Lucrezia.[15] On the deepest level, he perhaps reflects Machiavelli's abiding sense that eros always drives men outside their true selves and hence represents a threat to their identity. In his defining soliloquy, he sees himself suspended between Nicia's stupidity and Lucrezia's virtue and even foresees his own disappointment in the pleasure he so strongly desires. Echoing the words shared by Machiavelli and Vettori following the latter's prison ordeal, he urges himself to "face your lot." But unlike Machiavelli (and like Vettori himself), he is incapable of bearing his fate like a man, embracing instead a womanish passivity before the forces that assault him, as Lucrezia herself has already done with her mother and Fra Timoteo.

Ligurio, on the other hand, comes close to representing the arch-"Machiavellian" manipulator. We should be wary of dismissing Ligurio as a mere animator of events.[16] Machiavelli's trickster-parasite partakes of two paradigms: Rebhorn's ubiquitous "fox"—the con man *par excellence*—and a subtle constructor of reality. His quickness of wit is indisputable. Besides inventing the mandragola itself, he intuits the multiple virtues of a deaf Nicia and then tests his rival parasite Timoteo's friarly virtue by inventing a fictive abortion to earn Nicia's alms, whose amount he repeatedly ratchets up to torment the helplessly "deaf" Nicia. Then he executes a bait-and-switch to the real task of persuading Lucrezia to go through with the mandragola scheme, rendering the hapless Timoteo totally outclassed. Finally, he improvises a solution to the problem Callimaco has created in saying that he'll help the others nab the sacrificial victim (himself) to the potion by getting Timoteo to disguise himself as Callimaco. The mandragola itself is a kind of synecdoche for this dimension of his character. Its introduction underscores Ligurio's power to control others' reality, as well as framing his superiority as a con man.[17]

Ligurio seems to stand totally outside the events he is orchestrating. At one point, observing Callimaco nearly swoon in gratitude to Timoteo and Sostrata in anticipation of sexual pleasure, he apostrophizes, "What kind of person is this?" Yet he displays an insidious ability to enter into others' psyches. When Callimaco admits his distrust of the parasite, Ligurio counters that he can be trusted because "I desire you to satisfy this desire of yours almost as much as you do yourself." The implication is that Ligurio has the "negative capability" to easily imagine himself in another's skin. On the eve of Callimaco's triumph, Ligurio reminds him that once he gains Lucrezia's bed he'll still have to earn her complicity, even if it entails threatening her with scandal if she divulges the plot. Like Machiavelli in his device against the friars of Carpi, Ligurio takes evident pleasure in the sheer execution of the plot. He even manages to slip Nicia some foul-tasting camphor, in gratuitous payment for the latter's gullibility. After the trick, he shares in Callimaco's triumph, but nothing more is revealed about either his material reward for his part or his deeper satisfaction with its success.

Yet there are several implicit disclaimers of the Machiavellian ideal of disinterested amorality, as well as of the author's self-identification with his putative hero. Reflecting a Pirandello-like humanizing "sentiment of the contrary" at work in the text, it is Ligurio who in the finale thinks to ask if anyone will remember Siro.[18] In addition, Machiavelli seems more interested in Fra Timoteo's reactions to the events than in Ligurio's. The latter's acts are represented as aggressive without any hint of his author's own redemptive social purpose. For example, he makes no effort to deceive his audience.[19]

But, these qualifications aside, Ligurio does seem to embody something profoundly and quintessentially Machiavellian. If there is a positive ideal informing the parasite, it is a "writerly" one that centers in the power of fantasy to transcend the limitations of our fixed natures. Precisely because he operates imaginatively outside the arena of human actions and desires, Ligurio signifies the ultimate in human potentiality. As his name implies, Ligurio binds (*ligare*) the other personages into a new social order that reflects their true moral values. But in doing so he also implicitly gloats over (*ligurire*) them, fulfilling the threat of the two prologues. It is hard therefore to resist reading Ligurio's virtues as those of his author. Acknowledging the absence of ancient virtue in his fellow citizens, yet denied it himself by his evil fortune, in the person of Ligurio, Machiavelli exposes the whole instability and hollowness of their social and psychic orders. Far from empowering Lucrezia to seize the occasion and overthrow fortune, Ligurio subjects all of the play's characters to the "vulnerable posture of the early modern woman."[20]

The key to understanding the play may lie in the elusive mandragola itself. In addition to being a magic talisman by whose virtue one can rhetorically manipulate another's reality, Callimaco's potion is emblematic of the mysterious self, mirroring each character's beliefs, desires, and blindnesses. On those who control it, it bestows the gift of self-knowledge, sharing the power of the *Asino* lady's draft of evil. It is an elixir for the knowing that underscores the unique virtues of the literary imagination. Inoculated by reality, its true master is immune to its destructive power. By this final metamorphosis of the metaphoric *medicina* to the symbolic *mandragola*, Machiavelli the writer completes the transcendence of his personal misfortune through fantasy, producing at last an exemplar of the Machiavellian wise man.[21]

With *Clizia*, we return to the more conventional comic modality. However one rates the play's artistic merits, it is helpful to view Machiavelli's final comedy in the context of its precursors. Here he emphatically endorses those who adhere to a known identity as opposed to those who try to recreate themselves. The "hero" of the play is Sofronia, whose name ultimately derives from the Greek *sophron*, "of sound mind," and who successfully outmaneuvers both the aging reinvented lover, Nicomaco, and his conventional scheming steward, Eustachio.[22] As in *Mandragola*, while the young romantic male, Cleandro, gets the girl and satisfies his desires, he is not particularly admirable and wins virtually by default: his rival-father loses because his mother outwits them both. In the end, the moral of the play seems to be the conventional one of the folly of the superannuated lover; but in effect, Nicomaco's identity is preserved by his wife in spite of his own efforts to alter it, and he slinks into remorse and repentance.

The plot revolves around the familiar plight of the putative hero, Cleandro.[23] As he informs his friend Palamede in the opening scene, some twelve years earlier, in 1494, a gentleman-follower of the Count of Foix had sent his "booty," the five-year-old Clizia, to Cleandro's father. (At the time of the play, she is sixteen and Cleandro is twenty-one.) In time, Cleandro falls in love with her, but his parents keep her away from him; now his father, Nicomaco, loves her too and plots to marry Clizia to his servant Pirro, ensuring his own access to the girl. His jealous wife, Sofronia, opposing her husband's authority, would give her instead to their steward Eustachio. Nicomaco has rented the house of his neighbor, Damone, for Pirro and Clizia, while Cleandro orders Eustachio to clean up and prepare to marry. After complicated negotiations among father, mother, and son, a lottery turns out favorable to Nicomaco-Pirro. The old man prepares for the wedding of Clizia and Pirro, instructing the latter to take Clizia to Damone's house, where he'll substitute himself for the bridegroom. Pursuing her own remedy, Sofronia prompts Clizia's maid Doria to tell Nicomaco that Clizia is in a knife-wielding rage against him and Pirro. Ultimately humiliated in the bridal chamber by the substitution of the virile Siro for the bride, Nicomaco is brought back to himself. The intrigue is then resolved by the sudden arrival of Clizia's father, a Neapolitan gentleman named Ramondo, who easily persuades Nicomaco to let Clizia marry Cleandro in exchange for friendship between the two older men.

Throughout the play certain motifs recall Machiavelli's earlier comedies. The most obvious parallel is the transformed figure of the *senex*. The gull Nicia of *Mandragola* reappears in *Clizia* as the infatuated Nicomaco. But where Nicia's obsession with acquiring an heir establishes the basis for the device that will bring Callimaco to Lucrezia's bed, Nicomaco's infatuation with his ward explicitly threatens the entire order of his own household. From the outset we are asked to view this aberration as the old man's abrupt departure from a well-established personal identity, one that has been traced to Machiavelli's own infatuation with Barbara Raffacani Salutati (Nico-maco = Niccolò Machiavelli). The connection is borne out when Sofronia muses on Nicomaco's recent alteration. Her account of a typical day illustrating the "arrangement of his life" is a virtual parody of Machiavelli's in his famous letter to Vettori, except that it lacks the culminating bookish communion with the noble ancients. But now his fantasy about sleeping with Clizia has transformed him and wreaked chaos on the house.

Another link to the earlier comedies is the identity of the heroine. Like her counterpart in *Andria*, Clizia remains invisible. More than that, she functions as an "enclitic," inflecting the meaning of other characters' actions.[24] At various times she is described by others as knife-wielding, weeping, and so forth; and at one point we think we spy her, well-disguised, being bustled off to Damone's house for her tryst with Nicomaco. (It is, in fact, Siro.) But where in *Mandragola* Lucrezia emerges from her conventional nonentity as an at best equivocal female agent, in *Clizia* this role unequivocally belongs to Sofronia. Late in the play, Damone's wife, Sostrata, reminds the gentlemen of their power: "you've got the weapons. We're unarmed." But in fact, Nicomaco abuses the traditional patriarchal power by surrendering to eros, at one point even threatening to burn down his own house to demonstrate his authority. Conversely, though lacking patriarchal "arms," Sofronia and the other women are armed with superior wit, exercised in maintaining or restoring the subverted social order. Still, this order rests on the identity of Nicomaco, whom Sofronia has returned to himself. In contrast to the unresolved sexual and domestic disorder from which Fra Timoteo dispatches the audience at the conclusion of *Mandragola*, here it is Sofronia who dismisses the audience with the assurance that *this* wedding will be arranged "feminine, not masculine like that of Nicomaco."

Sofronia's ambiguous language alludes to both the female source of order and the unnatural coupling she has foiled. The latter is conveyed by the strong image Nicomaco has earlier conjured of Siro's "firm and pointy" thing menacing him from behind, when instead of Clizia he encounters his servant Siro standing "upright on the bed." In contrast to *Mandragola*'s structurally parallel image of the clueless Nicia feeling under the covers to assure himself of the lout's potency, that of Nicomaco's servant sodomically threatening his master implies the self-subverting power of the myth of sexual potency misapplied as the "staff" of rule in a declining social order. By reifying his phallic authority in a misguided self-rejuvenation, Nicomaco has threatened the natural order of things. Machiavelli drives home the menacing subversiveness of this move by transferring legitimate moral authority to the woman.

The emphasis on a natural social order founded on a natural sexual order underscores Sofronia's undermining of the patriarchal disorder of Nicomaco's plot. Only by returning her husband to "himself" can Sofronia live up to her name and reimpose wisdom in the state. At one point, Nicomaco suggests that he and Sofronia resolve their dispute by going to Fra Timoteo, "the confessor of our household," who had miraculously made pregnant the sterile Lucrezia. The authority of Sofronia, as well as the shifting moral perspective of the play, is made clear in her response: "Some great miracle" for a friar to make a woman pregnant; "I want to go to mass, and I don't want to submit my affairs to anyone." One is not likely to misread this as a gesture of piety. Rather than entrusting her business to another, especially those of a lascivious friar, Sofronia will maintain the appearance of piety while taking matters into her own hands.

By contrast with the centered Sofronia, not only the love-blinded Nicomaco, but also the young hero Cleandro is reduced to impotent passivity. In the disorder created by his father's infatuation, Cleandro feels himself buffeted by external forces. Torn between his parents' warring aims for dispensing of Clizia, he finds his natural filial piety at war with his own desires. Even after Nicomaco's defeat, he is tossed by "Fortune" from his father's love to his mother's ambition. His remedy, when it comes, appears in the person of Ramondo. Reverting to the conventionally comic *deus ex machina* of *Andria*, the appropriate mating of lover and ingénue is effected not by Sofronia's trick, but by a fortuitous external agent. But this echo serves only to reinforce Sofronia's crucial centeredness as well as the self-abandonment of Nicomaco. For while Ramondo reiterates Crito's functionality, he lacks his predecessor's moral warrant. It is not his character but merely the news he bears that authorizes the plot's resolution. The moral authority rests with Sofronia. Whether or not Machiavelli wishes to distance himself in *Clizia* from his own scornful temerity in *Mandragola*, it seems clear that his last, more morally conventional, comedy reasserts the strong sense of self often lamented in the quasi-tragic political-historical arena of *The Prince*, personally proclaimed in his letters, and confined to the morally ambiguous trickster Ligurio in *Mandragola*.[25]

In this chapter, I have tried to convey something of the nature and scope of Machiavelli's literary output. Given the fact that all of Machiavelli's important works date from the same period *post res perditas*, it is little more than a convenience to segregate his literary production from his better-known works of political theory. Once he found himself without an institutional outlet for the political savvy he had accumulated over fourteen years of service to Florence, writing became his only option, as well as a potential instrument for regaining access to power. It is always well to recall that the scandalous content of his most famous work, *The Prince*, ironically undercuts its professed (and unachieved) goal of earning him employment by the Medici. From 1512 on, Machiavelli was almost exclusively, and perforce, a writer, whether of discursive reflections on Italian princes and Roman magistrates or of poetic meditations on his own or Italy's fortunes— that is, whether as *istorico, comico* or *tragico*. It has been suggested, moreover, that Machiavelli is a great writer because he can embrace both the tragic limitations of reality to satisfy infinite human desire *and* the inchoate variety of things.[26] If there is any truth to this view, it is only appropriate that in ending with Machiavelli the writer we have returned to where we began.

Conclusion: Why Machiavelli Matters

Having sketched in the foregoing chapters Machiavelli's life and thought and the variety of forms in which he recorded them, I need to point out how they may be relevant to us in the twenty-first century. On one level, of course, no such justification is needed. Machiavelli is not an obscure figure clamoring to be exhumed from the dustbin of history. Instead, his name is a household word, the adjectival form of which denotes much that we identify with, and abhor in, our own political culture. Yet it is the very familiarity of the word *Machiavellian* and the contempt it breeds for politics as a whole that demands our attention to its creator. For if Machiavelli's reputation as a Machiavellian is deserved, it may well follow that he himself deserves to be forgotten as we struggle to purge ourselves of his nefarious influence. Clearly, I have written about him at this length because I believe this is not the case. Indeed, the informing conviction of this book is that Machiavelli *does* matter to our century, and that he has lessons to teach us that we sorely need to learn.

Surprisingly, Machiavelli's reputation over the centuries has been fairly consistently negative, though not always for the same reasons. In the century of his death, the Medici Grand Dukes of Tuscany found his very name to be "anathema."[1] Soon after *The Prince* was published posthumously in 1532, a consensus formed that has lasted for nearly half a millennium. However much they may have privately profited from his supposed teachings, political leaders and their followers agreed that "Machiavellism" was a pernicious disease infesting the body politic. In Shakespeare's time the demonic "stage Machiavel" achieved a scandalous popularity familiar to us in such villains as Richard III and Iago.

Though he was sporadically read, notably by Rousseau, as only ironically wicked—his bitter realism masking a deep commitment to democracy—Machiavelli's negative reputation has remained intact in our own time, and we have continued to regard him as quintessentially a "teacher of evil."[2] To be sure, this Straussian—or, as we would now say, "neocon"—take on Machiavelli's legacy has been increasingly challenged and modified in the last hundred years or so. But more often than not, even efforts to rehabilitate his reputation have focused on the liberating effect of his deeply cynical reading of politics, especially in *The Prince*, rather than on any kind of revisionist reconstruction of him as a seasoned and passionate republican.

To briefly recall Machiavelli's biography, it was his happy or unhappy lot to have lived at the height of turbulence in Renaissance Italy and Europe. Born at a time when de facto Medici domination of the city was morphing into open hegemony, he died a month after the Sack of Rome effectively ended any hope for Italian autonomy. At the midpoint of his fifty-eight-year life, Machiavelli began the brief period of his active involvement in republican politics. Although he produced many diplomatic documents during this time, and much of his poetry, it was only after the fall of the Republic and the restoration of Medici rule that he became preeminently a writer, virtually all of his best-known works having been produced between 1518 and 1525. Throughout his exile, he persisted in seeking reentry into the active life of politics, desiring to make the political wisdom he had gained during his years in the Chancery available to his countrymen. Except for a brief window of opportunity in 1525, this desire was largely frustrated, though the cataclysmic events of 1527 found him returning to Florence shortly before his death, too late to be reinstated in office.

Stepping back from the minutiae of his life and writings, we may well ask just what is the legacy that Machiavelli has bequeathed to us? Foremost is *Realpolitik*—that is, a hard-nosed, pragmatic approach to the practice of politics. Here I am thinking not so much of the scandal of "Machiavellism" as the analytical attention to practical motives that drive men (and, in his time, occasionally women) in the public sphere. Typical expressions of this quality are the long letters in which he calculates, with an almost mathematical precision, the pros and cons of various options facing the Pope, France, Germany, and others. This cold-blooded approach to politics is hardly the whole story of

Machiavelli's take on public life, and acknowledging it poses the risk of caricaturing him as a Machiavellian. But it is important nonetheless and should not be dismissed out of hand.[3]

One especially valuable product of Machiavelli's pragmatism is his body of reflections on the crisis that unfolded in his lifetime. Especially in his letters and dispatches, in the racier chapters of *The Prince*, and in the less well-known tracts he produced during these years, we find a valuable resource for understanding the threat posed by France, Spain, and the Hapsburg Empire to the traditional autonomy of the Italian states and to the republican heritage of his beloved Florence. Implicit in these ruminations—and particularly relevant to our own times—is a sustained argument for the superiority of active self-government by citizens in an age of incipient empire. Machiavelli was no wide-eyed idealist on this score; above all, he recognized and promoted the central role of a citizen militia in preserving republican institutions, a posture that, though virtually unique in his own time, arguably underpins our own still-lively debate about the meaning of the Second Amendment to the United States Constitution.

This broad overview of Machiavelli's legacy is fleshed out by the book's specific findings. Born near the end of the golden age of Florentine republicanism, his experience of citizen self-rule under the Soderini republic lasted from his twenty-ninth through his forty-third year, his remaining fifteen years being spent in uncomfortable exile under the suspicious Medici. His output can be roughly divided into the mostly practical reportage of his active years and the more familiar discursive writing of those following his downfall or, as he liked to say, *post res perditas*.

Among the former are the many reports sent home from the courts of France, Italy, Germany, and Rome. These letters and dispatches, as well as his major treatises, convey Machiavelli's complex views of republics and principalities. While the brunt of his production makes clear his own preference for republican government, which he explicitly proclaims as superior to the princely kind, his most important works leave us a record of his thoughtful reflections on both. Especially in *The Prince*, where he is writing as a republican about principalities, Machiavelli articulates the core of his philosophy: not the "Machiavellian" endorsement of brute force and deception, but his passion for military preparedness. The other key to his political philosophy is his understanding that princes and politicians are actors on a stage struggling to control men's minds in order to secure a regime that makes people happy.

A more straightforward expression of Machiavelli's republican ideals is presented in the *Discourses*. Here, contrasting the strength of the Roman Republic with the weaknesses of modern Florence and Italy, he develops a brief for republicanism. Specifically, he views class conflict as positive in Rome (though not always elsewhere) in that it helped foster institutional stability. Because the contending parties represented social classes with intrinsically divergent objectives, as opposed to what we would call the "special interests" of certain groups, the common goal was not the exclusive conquest of power as in Florence, but the continuity of the system.[4] Can the same be said of *our* political culture? We Americans are repeatedly enjoined from indulging in "class war," presumably because such an analysis springs from a historically disproved Marxism irrelevant to our conflictless polity. But it may be that we could arrive at a truer understanding of the legitimate opposed aims of different classes if we could learn from Machiavelli that such natural conflict may actually strengthen social stability.

Machiavelli bases his political theory on his anthropology. The universal desire for liberty dictates the suppression of individual appetites in the service of the common good, supplemented by such Machiavellian tenets as the need for rewards and punishments, the demand for severity, the channeling of wealth from individuals to the state, and the need for periodic renewal. Here, as always, war occupies a special place in his political thinking, and its exigencies dictate the diverse roles of virtue, religion, reputation, and fraud. The same qualities are exemplified, often by their absence, in the *Florentine Histories*, which present a modern case study to read against the idealized Roman model. While the history of his city yields examples of virtually all of the Machiavellian attributes of good and bad government, the crux for him is a citizen militia—in the final accounting, it is the "vileness" of war conducted by *condottieri*, he believes, that rendered the Italian states hostages to fortune.

At the heart of Machiavelli's reflections on statecraft is virtue. All of his political and historical works exemplify civic virtue and its lack. All public order depends on civic virtue, the cornerstone of which is individual virtue, whose absence from the contemporary scene is repeatedly contrasted with its abundance in ancient Rome. Virtue belongs to peoples as well as individuals, and nowhere is it more starkly manifested than in war, though religion can be an important contributor. Contextualized in a variety of ways, virtue and its absence have had profound effects on Roman and Italian history. In his more literary works, he dramatizes these effects, both positive and negative, perhaps most of all in the *Mandragola*.

In the philosophical arena, Machiavelli casts virtue in an epic struggle with fortune. His observations on this conflict run the gamut from a fatalistic view that fortune holds total sway in our lives to the opposite one that men should dominate fortune, with virtually every grade of resistance and collaboration in between. Crucial is the unrealizable ideal of shifting with fortune's changes or "turning one's face to fortune." Applying these precepts to history, ancient and modern, Machiavelli documents the role played by good and bad luck in the fortunes of states and individuals, itemizes her gifts to diverse peoples, examines how she favors some while ignoring others, and acknowledges misfortune as an inescapable part of life. Central to his teaching is the ratio of virtue to fortune, sometimes in relationships of collaboration, sometimes of opposition. His fascination with fortune is evident in his literary works, where her influence recurs with a quasi-superstitious regularity, reaching a kind of crescendo in his meditation in Chapter 5 of *L'Asino*.

The fact that we find such an important consummation in a literary work reminds us that for us Machiavelli is preeminently a writer. Apart from his famous riposte to Ariosto and his signature as "Niccolò Machiavelli *storico, comico, tragico*," the impressive body of writing that has come down to us justifies his self-definition. From his highly personal lyrics and his biting novella, *Belfagor*, to the always lively prose of his personal letters, the provocative satirical verse of *L'Asino*, and the diverse virtues of his comedies, especially *Mandragola*, Machiavelli demonstrates a lifelong commitment to the imaginative shaping of experience through language and form. In the service of a mind capable of penetrating the benign surface of events, he deployed a facility for transforming his insights into language (especially dialogue) that captures the essence of his world. If we wish to understand the Italian Renaissance, there are few guides as reliable—not to say delightful—as the author of *L'Asino* and *Mandragola*.

What can we learn from Machiavelli in the twenty-first century? It would be foolish to press the analogy too far between his era and our own. Machiavelli lived and worked in a small mixed republic in danger of being swallowed up by one of several national or supranational states vying for hegemony in Italy. Contemporary Americans belong to the sole surviving "superpower" in the aftermath of a similar power struggle that ended in 1989 with the collapse of the Soviet Union. Dominating the rest of the world militarily and, until recently, economically, the United States is the seat of a vast empire that influences, if it does not control, every corner of the world. To protect our interests and guarantee access to resources, especially in a time of imminent "peak oil," we disperse and at times have exercised our military might across the globe.

At such a critical juncture in the evolution (or is it devolution?) of our democracy, the posture adopted by ordinary citizens may well be determinative. Many believe that how Americans respond to George W. Bush's affirmation of autonomous executive power will decide whether or not the great experiment in representative self-government will survive. By the time you read these words his successor will have been elected. But few doubt that the degree of Bush's success in challenging our traditional system of checks and balances will spill over into succeeding administrations. The Iraq War, entering its sixth year as I write and with no clear exit-strategy in sight, poses perhaps the strongest challenge to popular government. From the outset, "Bush's war" has never enjoyed the support of a majority of Americans. Even as Congress was surrendering its constitutional responsibility to authorize going to war, millions of citizens took to the streets to demonstrate their opposition to the impending invasion of Iraq, and this despite a barrage of misinformation generated by a duplicitous White House and disseminated by a compliant media. As American (not to mention Iraqi) casualties mounted and the prospects for a spectral "victory" faded, this fundamental divide between a smugly self-confident president and a public alarmed by the deterioration of national prestige only increased. In the run-up to the 2008 election, as the foreign-policy debates among Democratic primary contenders and between them and a Republican nominee-in-waiting turn on the duration of our commitment to Iraq, the active engagement of citizens in the effort to curtail an unwarranted, disastrous "war of choice" has become crucial to the outcome.

Such a commitment to civic engagement must transcend any moral qualms we may have about the "public sphere." This brings us to the heart of Machiavelli's realism, the stark embrace of "effectual truth" that has alienated so many Christian and humanist readers. The only alternative to such realism is to abjure engagement altogether. In what remains the best single account of Machiavelli's teaching, Isaiah Berlin succinctly frames the choice we face:

> If you object to the political methods recommended [by Machiavelli] because they seem to you morally detestable, if you refuse to embark upon them because they are ... too frightening, Machiavelli has no answer, no argument. In that case you are perfectly entitled to lead a morally good life, be a private citizen (or a monk) [,] seek some corner of your own. But, in that event, you must not make yourself responsible for the life of others or expect good fortune; in a material sense you must expect to be ignored or destroyed. In other words you can opt out of the public world, but in that case he has nothing to say to you, for it is to the public world and to the men in it that he addresses himself.

Berlin goes on to argue that in discovering that there can be more than one system of values, Machiavelli challenges the assumption that somewhere there exists a definitive answer to the question of "how men should live," a disruption he sees as leading to both toleration and pluralism.[5] Throughout the preceding chapters, I have envisioned as my readers women and men who have opted to live in the public sphere and take collective responsibility for their lives.

In twenty-first-century America this can be a daunting challenge. It depends in large part on overcoming the influence of that well-financed expression of opinion that our courts have officially sanctioned as free speech. This feat, in turn, entails somehow curbing the influence of these moneyed interests on an increasingly concentrated media machine that propagates official dogma in the name of "news." Our reliance for such protection and information on courageous journalists, especially in marginal media instruments and on the Internet, is enormous. The fate of our democracy may well lie in the hands of a few dedicated reporters and bloggers willing to brook the lubrications of the powerful, and even to risk deliberate exclusion from the sources of information, in order to keep the public apprised of their leaders' real motives.

This imperative begins, but does not end, with a "Machiavellian" reading of both words and events. And while the exemplary skepticism of our designated interpreters of the public world can help us winnow the kernels of truth from the chaff of official chicanery and bluff, in the final analysis the burden of the task lies with us, the ordinary citizens who are their targets. Here too Machiavelli can be a formidable object of emulation. As with other models of conduct in the historical public sphere, we must profit from the example he provides us without succumbing to despair of ever reaching his level of efficacy. In his case this challenge is less daunting than in many. After all, Machiavelli is not Jesus, or Gandhi, or Martin Luther King. The example he sets is less one of heroic public activity than of a state of consciousness. Because he wrote, we are able to appreciate and even emulate that example. But in essence, Machiavelli matters to us because he provides a model of political *consciousness* as a means of informing whatever political *activity* our circumstances demand. One assumption of this book is that an appreciative reading of Machiavelli can help contemporary Americans summon up both the intellectual wherewithal and the political courage to resist the pressures we are under to exchange the responsibility of citizens for the compliance of subjects.

To be sure, there is a grim alternative to such a positive reception of Machiavelli. Whether we avail ourselves of the benefit of his teachings or not, our noble experiment in democracy may fail. In this case we can turn to him to sustain us, as he himself turned to the Romans to console himself for the failure of his contemporary Florentines to resist the Medici, and later of the Italians to fend off the Empire. By and large, however, we Americans are not a reflective lot, and we rightfully take pride in the exercise of active citizenship rather than (our vaunted piety notwithstanding) the enjoyment of private meditation. If we fail to preserve these freedoms, will our collective nature be miraculously transformed and America become a land of closet philosophers? Most of us would agree that such a metamorphosis would be better avoided, or best of all would take place without the collapse of our treasured liberties. But should the worst threats of our current situation be realized, we can always console ourselves with Machiavelli's example of the fortifying power of intellect and imagination when directed to our public life. At the very worst, in our post-republican phase we could emulate his bemused intelligence, smiling through our tears.

But, being Americans, we are inherently optimistic. And so our hope must be that the fruits of Machiavelli's democratic failure may help us to succeed. From its conception, the main argument of this book has been that Machiavelli is the seminal figure in early modern intellectual history for those living, or wishing to live, in a functional democracy. Persuaded by the "myth of Rome" that he developed during those years, he devised a powerful critique of Florence and of the failed Florentine Republic. But he also worked out in his writings a positive, even heroic, anthropology that underwrites his view of the proper posture of a citizen in a self-governing political community. While that posture is broad enough to entertain the traditional Machiavellian bugbears—the ends justify the means, one must learn to do evil by fusing the bestial and the human, and so forth—these are at best realistic nods to our flawed human nature. What makes Machiavelli indispensable to those of us living in and struggling to preserve a democracy is the sum of individual and collective qualities required of a citizen. For an age of "bowling alone" (in Robert Putnam's provocative phrase), Machiavelli sows through his works a powerful argument for an implicit model of free citizens working and struggling together to shape their common destiny.[6]

APPENDIX: MACHIAVELLI'S CIVIC TRACTS

A Discourse Made to the Magistracy of the Ten on Matters Relating to Pisa (1499)

Survey of the Things Done by the Florentine Republic to Calm the Parties in Pistoia (1501)

A Description of the Method Used by Duke Valentino in Killing Vitellozzo Vitelli, Oliverotto da Fermo, and Others (1502)

Words to Be Spoken Regarding the Provision of Money (1503)

A Discourse on Remodeling the Government of Florence (1506)

Report on Things Pertaining to Germany (1508; republished with a slightly different title in 1512)

Writing on the Way to Reconstitute the Regulation (between 1515–1519, also known as the *Ghiribizzi d'ordinanza*)

A Discourse on Florentine Matters after the Death of Lorenzo de' Medici the Younger (1520)

A Provision for the Institution of the Office of the Five Providers of the City Walls (1526)

An Exhortation to Penitence (probably 1526/1527).

NOTES

PREFACE

1. Naomi Wolf, *The End of America* (White River Junction, VT: Chelsea Green Publishing, 2007), p. 21 and passim.

CHAPTER 1

1. On the evolution of his family name, see Sebastian De Grazia, *Machiavelli in Hell* (Princeton, NJ: Princeton University Press, 1989), 209; on the activities of some of his forbears, Hannah Fenichel Pitkin, *Fortune Is a Woman* (Chicago: University of Chicago Press, 1999), 203f.

2. Ferdinand Schevill, *The Medici* (New York: Harper & Row, 1960), 5f.

3. Nicolai Rubinstein, "Machiavelli and Florentine Republican Experience," in G. Bock et al., *Machiavelli and Republicanism* (Cambridge: Cambridge University Press, 1990), 3–16.

4. J. H. Plumb, *The Italian Renaissance* (Boston: Houghton Mifflin, 1989), 63.

5. On Savonarola's reign, see Desmond Seward, *The Burning of the Vanities* (Stroud, UK: Sutton, 2006).

6. Respectively collected in *Legazioni e commissarie*, ed. S. Bertelli, 3 vols. (Milan: Feltrinelli, 1964), and the letters, *Machiavelli and His Friends: Their Personal Correspondence*, tr/ed. James B. Atkinson and David Sices (DeKalb: Northern Illinois University Press, 1996). Some of the former are translated in *Machiavelli, The Chief Works and Others*, ed. Allan Gilbert (Durham, NC: Duke University Press, 1989), vol. 1.

7. Machiavelli's untranslated reports from France are found in Machiavelli, *Opere scelte*, ed. G. F. Berardi (Rome: Editori Riuniti, 1973), 615–24.

8. Excerpts from these reports are translated in *Machiavelli, The Chief Works and Others*, ed. Allan Gilbert, 3 vols. (Durham, NC: Duke University Press, 1989). vol. I.

9. *Machiavelli, The Chief Works*, I.153.

10. On the controversy surrounding L. 121, see Roberto Ridolfi and Paolo Ghiglieri, "I *Ghiribizzi* al Soderini," *La bibliofilia* 72(1970): 53–74.

11. John M. Najemy, "The Controversy Surrounding Machiavelli's Service to the Republic," in *Machiavelli and Republicanism*, 101–17, asserts that for Machiavelli, writing letters and reports was "a matter of inner need" that, while it left him isolated, also "opened up horizons of theory and history … inaccessible … to a more conventional chancery secretary."

12. Robert Black, "Machiavelli, Servant of the Florentine Republic," in *Machiavelli and Republicanism*, 71–99. Black believes that the aristocrats' suspicion of his partisanship after the restoration may have been misplaced, his dismissal expressing the aristocrats' hatred of the whole "notarial class."

13. Roberto Ridolfi, *The Life of Niccolò Machiavelli*, tr. Cecil Grayson (Chicago: University of Chicago Press, 1963), 165, designates 1513–1519 as Machiavelli's "literary" period, encompassing Machiavelli's best-known works, as well as the *Dialogo intorno alla nostra lingua*. Blasucci dates the *Dialogo* from 1524.

14. Atkinson and Sices conjecture that Machiavelli was disappointed in this response, especially in light of Vettori's enthusiasm for his friend's letters a few paragraphs later, *Machiavelli and His Friends*, 518.

15. A full account of the Riccia affair is given in Viroli, *Niccolò's Smile*, 161–64.

16. Ardinghelli's letter is quoted at length by Ridolfi, *Life*, 162.

17. Ridolfi, *Life*, 173–75, conjectures that the play was produced to celebrate the return of Lorenzo with his French bride on September 7, 1518. Though the dates—and in the case of the *Dialogo*, even the authorship—of *Belfagor* and the *Dialogo intorno alla nostra lingua* are uncertain, it is possible that he composed both works at this time.

18. In Letter 286 (February 22, 1525), Machiavelli's friend Filippo de' Nerli records the success and resulting fame of Machiavelli's comedies at Modena. For a full account of Machiavelli's love affairs, see De Grazia, 122–31; for a penetrating analysis of his (self)presentation(s) as a lover, see Guido Ruggiero, *Machiavelli in Love* (Baltimore: Johns Hopkins University Press, 2007), 108–62.

19. According to the novelist Bandello, he humiliated himself in the duke's presence by trying to parade an infantry company; see Maurizio Viroli, *Niccolò's Smile: A Biography of Machiavelli*, tr. Antony Shugaar (New York: Farrar Straus and Giroux, 2000), 241.

20. On Machiavelli's relations with the chancery and his alleged "antagonism" with its humanist culture, see Peter Godman, *From Poliziano to Machiavelli: Florentine Humanism in the High Renaissance* (Princeton, NJ: Princeton

University Press, 1998), 275–86. For a more "humanistic" Machiavelli, see Werner Gundersheimer, "San Casciano, 1513: A Machiavellian Moment," *Journal of Medieval and Renaissance Studies* 17:1(1987): 41–58.

21. Some sources give his date of death as June 20.

CHAPTER 2

1. Citations of Machiavelli's letters in the original are from Machiavelli, *Lettere*, in *Opere di Niccolò Machiavelli: Scritti letterari* (vol. 3), ed. Franco Gaeta (Turin: UTET, 1984); translations are from *Machiavelli and His Friends*. They will be referred to in the text by their numbers, which are identical in both editions.

2. The complete *Legazioni* comprise more pages than *The Prince* and *Discourses* combined. I limit my comments here to the selections in Machiavelli, *Opere scelte*, ed. G. F. Berardi (Rome: Editori Riuniti, 1973) and those translated by Allan Gilbert, in *Machiavelli, The Chief Works and Others* (Durham, NC: Duke University Press, 1989), v. 1. Translations from Berardi that Gilbert does not include are my own.

3. Noting that the now-proverbial expression was attributed by Commynes to Pope Alexander VI, Berardi cites Chapter 12 of *The Prince*, where Machiavelli says that Charles VIII of France "was allowed to take Italy with chalk" (618n.).

4. On returning to Florence the following month, Machiavelli described these events more fully in his *Description of the Method Used by Duke Valentino in Killing Vitellozzi Vitelli, Oliverotto da Fermo.*

5. When he reflects on these events six or seven years later in *Discourses* I.27, Machiavelli is somewhat harsher, attributing Baglioni's acts to cowardice and "vileness." The third, and by far most notorious, of Machiavelli's responses to these events is his letter of September 13–21 (L. 121), the famous *Ghiribizzi*; for which, see below, p. 38.

6. *Palle* refers to the six red balls on a gold field on the Medici coat of arms. In his later account of these events in *Discourses* II.27, Machiavelli implies that the situation may have been saved had Soderini more quickly agreed to Cardona's proposal (*Machiavelli and His Friends*, 495f.). For Machiavelli's "belief that Soderini's fatal flaw was his inability to act decisively" (Ibid., 496), see the epitaph cited above in Chapter 1, p. 15.

7. Machiavelli is perhaps being a bit oversensitive here. Tucci's letter (L. 82, November 21, 1503) arguably implies no such criticism.

8. On this letter see pp. 20 and 25, above.

9. *Machiavelli and His Friends*, 466.

10. For Machiavelli's various missions and his role in conducting Florentine foreign policy from 1498–1512, see Sergio Bertelli, "Machiavelli e la politica esterna fiorentina," in *Studies on Machiavelli*, 29–72.

11. It should be noted that of the 203 letters from the same period collected in the standard UTET edition and its predecessors, only 16 are *by* Machiavelli, as opposed to 66 of 132 letters dating from after the "fall."

12. Machiavelli was sufficiently impressed to "tarry" at Mantua or Bologna until January 2, 1510; *Machiavelli and His Friends*, 489.

13. *Machiavelli and His Friends*, xviii.

14. Cascina is a town a few miles east of Pisa. Ridolfi, 107, notes that the militia "recognized his authority more than that of the commissioners" (cited in *Machiavelli and His Friends*, 489n.).

15. See Inglese's review of *Opere: Lettere*, ed. Gaeta, in *La Bibliografia* 86 (1984): 271–80; cited in *Machiavelli and His Friends*, 468.

16. The translators note that "the sensory element [of *gustare*] suggests intuition as well as mental effort in such consideration" (Ibid., 469n.).

17. Gaeta, *Lettere*, 241n.

CHAPTER 3

1. Niccolai Rubinstein, "Machiavelli and the World of Florentine Politics," in *Studies on Machiavelli*, 3–28.

2. *The Prince*, tr./ed. Robert M. Adams (New York: W. W. Norton & Co., 1992). All citations of the work in English are to this edition.

3. The *terminus ad quem* is Machiavelli's famous letter to Vettori (L. 224, December 10, 1513), in which he first announces that he has "composed a short study, *De principatibus*."

4. Roberto Ridolfi, *The Life of Niccolò Machiavelli*, tr. Cecil Grayson (Chicago: University of Chicago Press, 1963), 148, 154. For an argument that the *Discourses* were written without interruption in late 1517, see J. H. Whitfield, "Considerazioni pratiche sui *Discorsi*," in *Studies on Machiavelli*, 361–69.

5. Quoted by Maurizio Virolli, *Niccolò's Smile: A Biography of Machiavelli*, tr. Antony Shugaar (New York: Farrar Straus and Giroux, 2000), 115.

6. Leo Strauss, *Thoughts on Machiavelli* (University of Chicago Press, 1958), 9. The Straussian line is further developed by Harvey C. Mansfield in *Machiavelli's Virtue* (Chicago: University Chicago Press, 1996).

7. Tiziano Perez, "*Reputazione* in Machiavelli's Thought," in *Machiavelli: Figure-Reputation* (= *Yearbook of European Studies/Annuaire d'Études Europeennes* 8], ed. Joep Leerssen and Menno Spiering (Amsterdam and Atlanta: Rodopi, 1996), 165–78. Cf. Gerald Svez, "The Enigma of the Political Stage Director," *SubStance* 25(1996): 3–45.

8. According to Pocock, *The Machiavellian Moment*, 333, the essence of Machiavellism is (1) the revision of *virtù* as a "theory of arms as essential to liberty"; (2) an Aristotelian-Polybian theory of mixed government in which Venice was "both paradigm and myth"; and (3) concepts of custom, apocalypse, and *anakuklosis* (revolution) based on "use, faith, and fortune."

9. Luigi Derla, "Machiavelli moralista," *Italianistica* 10(1981): 21–35. Cf. Maurizio Viroli, "Machiavelli and the Republican Idea of Politics," in G. Bock et al., *Machiavelli and Republicanism* (Cambridge University Press, 1990), pp. 143–72.

10. Peter S. Donaldson, *Machiavelli and Mystery of State* (Cambridge University Press, 1988), reads *The Prince* and *Discourses* as evidence that Machiavelli was "the reviver or reviser of an ancient mystery of statecraft" (ix).

11. Donald Weinstein, "Machiavelli and Savonarola," in *Studies on Machiavelli*, 251–64; Guido Pampaloni, "Il Movimento Piagnone secondo la Lista del 1497," *Studies on Machiavelli*, 335–48.

12. See, among others, Cary J. Nederman, "Amazing Grace, Fortune, God, and Free Will in Machiavelli's Thought," *Journal of the History of Ideas* 60(1999): 617–38.

13. Nicola Matteucci, "Nicoolò Machiavelli Politologo," *Studies on Machiavelli*, 207–48.

14. Quentin Skinner, "Machiavelli's *Discorsi* and the Pre-humanist Origins of Republican Ideas," in G. Bock et al., *Machiavelli and Republicanism*, 140f. For Jefferson's similar views on periodic renewal, see Gore Vidal, *Inventing a Nation: Washington, Adams, Jefferson* (New Haven and London: Yale University Press, 2003), 32 and 166.

15. For an argument that the *Histories* were intended to "demonstrate the abasement of Florentine political life under the Medici" (86), see Felix Gilbert, "Machiavelli's *Istorie fiorentine*: An Essay in Interpretation," in *Studies on Machiavelli*, 73–99.

16. Gisella Bock, "Civil Discord in Machiavelli's *Istorie Fiorentine*," in G. Bock et al., *Machiavelli and Republicanism*, 181–201.

17. This florescence is still visible today in the look of the city. In the ensuing peace of 1298, the foundation of the Palazzo Vecchio and the Piazza della Signoria were laid.

CHAPTER 4

1. See, for example, Harvey Mansfield, *Machiavelli's Virtue* (Chicago: University of Chicago Press, 1996).

2. John Plamenetz, "In Search of Machiavellian *Virtù*," in Anthony Parel, ed., *The Political Calculus* (Toronto: University of Toronto Press, 1972), 157–78;

and Neal Wood, "Machiavelli's Concept of *Virtù* Reconsidered," *Political Studies* 15(1967): 159–72.

3. J. H. Whitfield, "On Machiavelli's Use of *Ordini*," *Italian Studies* 10(1955): 19–39.

4. Anthony J. Parel, *The Machiavellian Cosmos* (New Haven: Yale University Press, 1992), 87–100.

5. *Machiavelli: Il teatro e tutti gli scritti letterari*, ed. Franco Gaeta (Milan: Feltrinelli, 1977); tr. *Lust and Liberty: The Poems of Machiavelli*, tr. Joseph Tusiani (New York: Ivan Obolonsky, Inc., 1963), with slight modifications of my own. Unless otherwise noted, subsequent quotes of the poems in English are from this translation.

6. I have taken the liberty of adjusting Tusiani's translations in a few details.

7. Along with Lorenzo, Duke of Urbino, Giuliano is immortalized by Michelangelo in the figures of Day and Night [or "action" and "reflection"] in the New Sacristy of the church of San Lorenzo in Florence.

8. The Italian text is from Gaeta, *Teatro*; translations are by Mera J. Flaumenhaft, *Mandragola* (Prospect Heights, IL: Waveland Press, 1981).

9. The following paragraphs are condensed from my "Writing and the Paradox of the Self: Machiavelli's Literary Vocation," *RQ* 59(2006): 59–89.

10. Wayne A. Rebhorn, *Foxes and Lions: Machiavelli's Confidence Men* (Ithaca, NY: Cornell University Press, 1988), 67.

11. Tr. Daniel T. Gallagher (Prospect Heights, IL: Waveland Press, 1996), 22.

CHAPTER 5

1. Valla, "Dialogue on Free Will," tr. Charles E. Trinkaus Jr., in *The Renaissance Philosophy of Man*, ed. Ernst Cassirer *et al.* (Chicago: University of Chicago Press, 1961), 155–82.

2. Gaeta, *Teatro*; translations are from *Clizia*, tr. Daniel T. Gallagher (Prospect Heights, IL: Waveland Press, 1996).

3. Thomas Flanagan, "The Concept of *Fortuna* in Machiavelli," in *The Political Calculus*, ed. Anthony Parel (Toronto: University of Toronto Press, 1972), 137–54.

4. See Hanna F. Pitkin, *Fortune Is a Woman: Gender and Politics in the Thought of Niccolò Machiavelli* (Berkeley and Los Angeles: University of California Press, 1984).

5. Ezio Raimondi, "Arte dello stato e *ghiribizzi* dell'esistenza," in *Politica e commedia; dal Beroaldo al Machiavelli*. (Bologna: Il Mulino, 1972), 141–63 (154).

6. Anthony J. Parel, *The Machiavellian Cosmos* (New Haven, CT: Yale University Press, 1992), 64.

7. The Renaissance Italian *capitolo* (= "chapter") is "a single autonomous poem," usually in terza rima written in imitation of Dante's cantos in the *Divine Comedy*; see Valerie Masson de Goméz, "The Vicissitudes of the *Capitolo* in Spain," *Pacific Coast Philology* 16(981): 57. Of Machiavelli's four capitoli, three are from 187–93, the fourth ("L'Occasione") 21 lines in length.

8. Victoria Kahn, *Rhetoric, Prudence, and Skepticism in the Renaissance* (Ithaca, NY: Cornell University Press, 1985), 70.

9. Richard Greenwood, "Machiavelli and the Problem of Human Inflexibility," in *The Cultural Heritage of the Italian Renaissance: Essays in Honour of T. G. Griffith*, ed. C. E. J. Giffiths and R. Hastings (Lewiston, NY: Mellen, 1993), 196–214.

10. Charles D. Tarlton, "*Fortuna* and the Landscape of Action in Machiavelli's *Prince*," *New Literary History* 30(1999): 737–55.

11. Timothy J. Lukes, "Fortune Comes of Age (in Machiavelli's Literary Works)," *SCJ* 11(1980): 33–50.

12. What the Italian more literally says is that they could easily have "shown again their face to fortune" and thus attained more glorious or honorable results.

13. See Chapter 6, and my essay "Writing and the Paradox of the Self: Machiavelli's Literary Vocation," *Renaissance Quarterly* 59(2006): 59–89.

14. Donald A. Beecher, "Machiavelli's *Mandragola* and the Emerging Animateur," *Quaderni d'Italianistica* 5(1984): 171–89.

15. Francesca R. Sparacio, "Il processo del comico ne *La Mandragola* di Niccolò Machiavelli," *Romance Review* 5(1995): 73–5, concludes that in *Mandragola* various characters advance the plot's comicity by modifying its events to "reveal the play of the forces of *fortuna* and *virtù*" (82).

16. Throughout this discussion, quotes of Machiavelli's poems have been from *Lust and Liberty: The Poems of Machiavelli*, tr. Joseph Tusiani (New York: Ivan Obolonsky, Inc., 1963). Here, however, I have substituted a literal translation of "il voler di fortuna" for Tusiani's "the things that must indeed be done" (p. 76).

17. See Murizio Viroli, *Machiavelli's Smile*, tr. Antony Shugaar (New York: Farrar, Straus and Giroux, 2000).

CHAPTER 6

1. Richard C. Clark, "Machiavelli: Bibliographical Spectrum," *Italy: Machiavelli "500"* [= *Review of National Literatures* 1 (1970)]; Carlo Dionisotti, "Machiavelli, Man of Letters," in *Machiavelli and the Discourse of Literature*, ed. Albert Russell Ascoli and Victoria Kahn (Cornell University Press, 1993), 16–51. Lanfranco Caretti, "Machiavelli scrittore," *Terzoprogramma* 1(1970): 49–57,

finds "no clear demarcation between the political Machiavelli and Machiavelli the author" (50).

2. Albert Russell Ascoli, "Ariosto and the 'Fier Pastor': Form and History in *Orlando Furioso*," *Renaissance Quarterly* 54(2001): 487–522.

3. See the Appendix for a list of these works.

4. Ettore Bonora, "Qualche proposta per il testo e il commento del capitolo di fortuna del Machiavelli," *GSLI* 105(1988): 321–36.

5. The strambottto is an ancient verse-form, originally from Sicily, composed of a single stanza of either six or eight eleven-syllable lines.

6. Arlene W. Saxonhouse, "Comedy, Machiavelli's Letters, and His Imaginary Republics," in *The Comedy and Tragedy of Machiavelli: Essays on the Literary Works*, Vickie B. Sullivan, ed. (New Haven and London: Yale University Press, 2000), 57–77 (59).

7. Guido Ruggiero, "Machiavelli in Love," in *Machiavelli in Love* (Baltimore: Johns Hopkins University Press, 2007), 108–62; cf. Juliana Schiesari, "Libidinal Economies: Machiavelli and Fortune's Rape," in *Desire in the Renaissance: Psychoanalysis and Literature*, Valeria Finucci and Regina Schwartz, eds. (Princeton, NJ: Princeton University Press, 1994), 169–83.

8. See John M. Najemy, *Between Friends: Discourses of Power and Desire in the Machiavelli-Vettori Letters of 1513–1515* (Princeton, NJ: Princeton University Press, 1993). In an oral communication, Guido Ruggiero has pointed out to me that Machiavelli has slyly reversed the sexual preferences of his two friends.

9. Brian Richardson, "Two Notes on Machiavelli's *Asino*," *BHR* 40(1978): 137–41; Luigi Blasucci, "Machiavelli novelliere e verseggiatore," *Cultura e scuola* 33/34(1970): 174–91; Michael Harvey, "Lost in the Wilderness: Love and Longing in *L'Asino*," in *The Comedy and Tragedy of Machiavelli*, 120–37.

10. Giulio Ferroni, "Appunti sull'*Asino* di Machiavelli," in *Letteratura e critica: studi in onore di Natalino Sapegno* (1975), 313–45 (326); see also Gian Mario Anselmi, "L'Altro Machiavelli," in Anselmi and Paolo Fazion, *Machiavelli: L'Asino e le bestie* (Bologna: CLUEB, 1984), 9–23; and the various interpretations in Gian Mario Anselmi and P. Fazion, ed. *Machiavelli: L'Asino e le bestie* (Bologna: CLUEB, 1984). For an overall assessment of Machiavelli's verse-narratives, including the *Decennali*, see Giorgio Bàrberi-Squarotti, "Storia e etica in versi: il tono medio del Machiavelli," *Italianistica* 2(1974): 15–32

11. Giorgio Inglese, "Postille machiavelliane," *La cultura* 23(1985), 235f.

12. "*Andria*: The Woman from Andros," original text and translation by James B. Atkinson, in *The Comedies of Machiavelli*, ed. David Sices and James B. Atkinson (Hanover, NH: University Presses of New England, 1985), 41–51.

13. See Harvey Mansfield, "The Cuckold in *Mandragola*," in *The Comedy and Tragedy of Machiavelli*, 1–29; and Robert Palmer and James F. Pontuso,

"The Master Fool: The Conspiracy of Machiavelli's *Mandragola*," *Perspectives on Political Science* 25(1996): 124–31.

14. Joseph A. Barber, "The Irony of Lucrezia," *Studies in Philology* 82(1985): 450–9; Ronald L. Martinez, "The Pharmacy of Machiavelli: Roman Lucretia in *Mandragola*," *Renaissance Drama* 14(1983): 1–43; Susan Behuniak-Long, "The Significance of Lucrezia in Machiavelli's *La Mandragola*," *Review of Politics* 51: 264–83; Franco Tonelli, "Machiavelli's *Mandragola* and the Signs of Power," in *Drama, Sex, and Politics*, ed. James Redmond (Cambridge: Cambridge University Press, 1985), 35–54; Carnes Lord, "Allegory in Machiavelli's *Mandragola*," in *Political Philosophy and the Human Soul*, ed. M. Palmer and T. Pangle (Lanham, MD: Rowman & Littlefield, 1994), 152–67.

15. Salvatore di Maria, "The Ethical Premises for the *Mandragola*'s New Society," *Italian Culture* 7(1986–89): 17–33.

16. As does Giulio Ferroni in "Le 'cose vane' nelle *Lettere* di Machiavelli," *La rassegna della letteratura italiana* 76(1972): 215–64; cf. Ferroni, *"Mutazione" e "riscontro" nel teatro di Machiavelli e altri saggi sulla commedia del Cinquecento* (Rome: Bulzoni, 1972), 68.

17. Joseph A. Barber, "La strategia linguistica di Ligurio nella *Mandragola* di Machiavelli," *Italianistica* 13(1984): 387–95; Francesca R. Sparacio, "Il processo del comico ne *La Mandragola* di Niccolò Machiavelli," *Romance Review* 5:1(1995): 73–85; Franco Fido, "Machiavelli 1469–1969: Politica e Teatro nel Badalucco di Messer Nicia," *Italica* 46(1969): 359–75; and Roberto Giraldi, "Machiavelli's *Mandragola*: The Root of Revelry or Rebeldry?" *Canadian Journal of Italian Studies* 15(1992): 17–28.

18. Franco Masciandaro, "Machiavelli umorista," *Il Veltro* 40(1995): 190–95 (194).

19. Donald Beecher, "Machiavelli's *Mandragola* and the Emerging Animateur," *Quaderni d'Italianistica* 5(1984): 171–78.

20. Jane Tylus, "Theater and Its Social Uses: Machiavelli's *Mandragola* and the Spectacle of Infamy," *Renaissance Quarterly* 53(2000): 656–83 (676).

21. Paolo Baldan, "Sulla vera natura della *Mandragola*," *Il Ponte* 34(1978): 387–407.

22. See Catherine Zuckert, "Fortune Is a Woman—But So Is Prudence: Machiavelli's *Clizia*," in *Finding a New Feminism: Rethinking the Woman Question for Liberal Democracy*, ed. Pamela Jensen (Lanham, MD: Rowman & Littlefield, 1996), 24–35; Martin Fleischer, "Trust and Deceit in Machiavelli's Comedies," *Journal of the History of Ideas* 27(1966): 368–74; and Salvatore Di Maria, "Nicomaco and Sofronia: Fortune and Desire in Machiavelli's *Clizia*," *Sixteenth-Century Journal* 14(1983): 201–13.

23. Machiavelli, *Clizia*, tr. Daniel T. Gallagher (Prospect Heights, IL: Waveland Press, 1996).

24. Ronald L. Martinez, "Benefit of Absence: Machiavellian Valediction in *Clizia*," in *Machiavelli and the Discourse of Literature*, 117–44.

25. Carlo Dionisotti, "Appunti sulla *Mandragola*," *Belfagor* 39(1984): 621–24 (638). Robert Faulkner, *"Clizia* and the Enlightenment of Private Life," *The Comedy and Tragedy of Machiavelli*, 30–56; see also Franco Ferrucci, "Anthropologia machiavelliana," *Annali d'italianistica* 15(1997): 99–108; and Carmela Pesca-Cupolo, *"La Clizia* come meditazione senile di Machiavelli," *Forum Italicum* 28(1994): 252–68.

26. Joseph Anthony Mazzeo, "The Poetry of Power," *Italy: Machiavelli "500"* [= *Review of National Literatures* 1(1970)].

CONCLUSION

1. J. R. Hale, *Florence and the Medici* (London: Phoenix Press, 2004 [1977]), 158.

2. Strauss; see above, p. 1 and passim.

3. On the narrower issue of Machiavelli's "humanism," see, in addition to the works of Strauss and Mansfield cited in Chapter 3, Mark Hulliung, *Citizen Machiavelli* (Princeton, NJ: Princeton University Press, 1983), esp. pp. 237f.

4. Nicola Matteucci, "Niccolò Machiavelli Politologo," in *Studies on Machiavelli*, 207–48.

5. Isaiah Berlin, "The Originality of Machiavelli," in *Studies on Machiavelli*, 147–206.

6. Robert D. Putnam, *Bowling Alone: The Collapse and Revival of American Community* (New York: Simon & Schuster, 2000).

BIBLIOGRAPHY

MONOGRAPHS

Andrews, Richard. *Scripts and Scenarios: The Performance of Comedy in Renaissance Italy* (Cambridge: Cambridge University Press, 1993).

Anglo, Sydney. *Machiavelli: A Dissection* (New York: Harcourt, Brace & World, 1969).

Barberi-Squarotti, Giorgio. *La forma tragica del 'Principe' e altri saggi sul Machiavelli.* (Florence: Olschki, 1966).

Bonadeo, Alfredo. *Corruption, Conflict, and Power in the Works and Times of Niccolò Machiavelli* (Berkeley: University of California Press, 1973).

Cavallini, Giorgio. *Interpretazione della Mandragola* (Milan: Marzorati, 1973).

Chabod, Federico. *Machiavelli and the Renaissance*, tr. David Moore (New York: Harper & Row, 1958).

———. *Scritti su Machiavelli* (Turin: Einaudi, 1964).

Cope, Jackson I. *Secret Sharers in Italian Comedy: From Machiavelli to Goldoni* (Durham, NC: Duke University Press, 1996).

De Grazia, Sebastian. *Machiavelli in Hell* (Princeton, NJ: Princeton University Press, 1989).

De Maria, Udo. *Intorno ad un Poema Satirico di Niccolò Machiavelli* (Bologna: Zamorani e Albertazzi, 1899).

Dionisotti, Carlo. *Machiavellerie: Storia e fortuna di Machiavelli* (Turin: Einaudi, 1980).

Donaldson, Peter S. *Machiavelli and Mystery of State* (Cambridge: Cambridge University Press, 1988).

Ferroni, Giulio. *"Mutazione" e "riscontro" nel teatro di Machiavelli e altri saggi sulla commedia del Cinquecento* (Rome: Bulzoni, 1972).

Fido, Franco. *Machiavelli* (Palermo: Palumbo, 1965).

———. *Le metamorfosi del centauro: Studi e letture da Boccaccio a Pirandello* (Rome: Bulzoni, 1977).

Flaumenhaft, Mera J. *The Civic Spectacle* (Lanham, MD: Rowman & Little-field, 1994).

Fleisher, Martin, ed. *Machiavelli and the Nature of Political Thought* (New York: Atheneum, 1972).

Fontana, Benedetto. *Hegemony and Power: On the Relation between Gramsci and Machiavelli* (Minneapolis: University of Minnesota Press, 1993).

Garosci, Aldo. *Le "Istorie fiorentine" del Machiavelli* (Turin: Giappichelli, 1973).

Garver, Eugene. *Machiavelli and the History of Prudence* (Madison: University of Wisconsin Press, 1987).

Gilbert, Allan. *Machiavelli's "Prince" and Its Forerunners* (Durham, NC: Duke University Press, 1938).

Gilbert, Felix. *Machiavelli and Guicciardini: Politics and History in Sixteenth-Century Florence* (Princeton, NJ: Princeton University Press, 1965).

Godman, Peter. *From Poliziano to Machiavelli: Florentine Humanism in the High Renaissance* (Princeton, NJ: Princeton University Press, 1998).

Guillemain, Bernard. *Machiavel: L'Anthropologie politique* (Geneva: Droz, 1977).

Hulliung, Mark. *Citizen Machiavelli* (Princeton, NJ: Princeton University Press, 1983).

Kahn, Victoria. *Rhetoric, Prudence, and Skepticism in the Renaissance* (Ithaca, NY: Cornell University Press, 1985).

————. *Machiavellian Rhetoric: From the Counter-Reformation to Milton* (Princeton, NJ: Princeton University Press, 1994).

Landucci, Luca. *A Florentine Diary from 1450 to 1516*, tr. Alice de Rosen Jervis (London: J. M. Dent, 1927).

Machiavelli, Niccolò. *Belfagor arcidiavolo* (Genoa: Il Melangolo, 1982).

————. *Clizia*, tr. Daniel T. Gallagher (Prospect Heights, IL: Waveland Press, 1996).

————. *The Comedies of Machiavelli* (bilingual ed.), ed./tr. David Sices and James B. Atkinson (Hanover, NH: University Presses of New England, 1985).

————. *Discorsi sopra la prima deca di Tito Livio*, ed. Giorgo Inglese (Milan: Rizzoli, 1984).

————. *The Discourses*, tr. Leslie J. Walker (London: Penguin Books, 1983 [1970]).

————. *Erotica*, ed. Gerolamo Lazzeri. (Milan: Dall' Oglio, n.d.).

————. *Florentine Histories*, tr. Laura F. Banfield and Harvey C. Mansfield, Jr. (Princeton, NJ: Princeton University Press, 1988).

————. *Legazioni e commissarie*, ed. S. Bertelli, 3 vols. (Milan: Feltrinelli, 1964).

————. *Lettere*, ed. Franco Gaeta (Milan: Feltrinelli, 1981 [1961]).

————. *Lettere*, in *Opere di Niccolò Machiavelli: Scritti letterari* (v. 3), ed. Franco Gaeta (Turin: UTET, 1996 [1989]).

————. *Lust and Liberty: The Poems of Machiavelli*, tr. Joseph Tusiani (New York: Ivan Obolonsky, Inc., 1963).

————. *Machiavelli: The Chief Works and Others*, ed. Allan Gilbert, 3 vols. (Durham, NC: Duke University Press, 1989).

————. *Machiavelli. Il teatro e tutti gli scritti letterari*, ed. Franco Gaeta (Milan: Feltrinelli, 1977 [1965]).

————. *Machiavelli and His Friends: Their Personal Correspondence*, tr/ed. James B. Atkinson and David Sices (DeKalb: Northern Illinois University Press, 1996).

————. *Mandragola*, ed. G. Sasso and G. Inglese (Milan: Rizzoli, 1980).

————. *Mandragola*, tr. Mera J. Flaumenhaft (Prospect Heights, IL: Waveland Press, 1981).

————. *Novella di Belfagor, L'Asino*, ed. M. Tarantino (Rome: Salerno, 1990).

————. *Opere di Niccolò Machiavelli: Scritti letterari* (v. 4), ed. Luigi Blasucci (Turin: UTET, 1996 [1989]).

————. *Opere scelte*, ed. G. F. Berardi (Rome: Editori Riuniti, 1973).

————. *Il prinicipe*, ed. Franco Melotti and Ettore Janni (Milan: Rizzoli, 1982).

Mansfield, Harvey C. *A Study of the "Discourses on Livy"* (Ithaca, NY: Cornell University Press, 1979).

————. *Machiavelli's Virtue* (Chicago: University of Chicago Press, 1996).

Martelli, Mario. *Machiavelli e gli storici antichi* (Rome: Salerno, 1998).

Mattei, Rodolfo de. *Dal premachiavellismo all'antimachiavellismo* (Florence: Sansoni, 1969).

McCanles, Michael. *The Discourse of "Il Principe"* (Malibu, CA: Undena Publications, 1983).

Najemy, John M. *Between Friends: Discourses of Power and Desire in the Machiavelli-Vettori Letters of 1513–1515* (Princeton, NJ: Princeton University Press, 1993).

Parel, Anthony J. *The Machiavellian Cosmos* (New Haven, CT: Yale University Press, 1992).

Pitkin, Hanna F. *Fortune Is a Woman: Gender and Politics in the Thought of Niccolò Machiavelli* (Berkeley and Los Angeles: University of California Press, 1984).

Plumb, J. H. *The Italian Renaissance* (Boston: Houghton Mifflin, 1989 [1961]).

Pocock, J. G. A. *The Machiavellian Moment: Florentine Political Thought and the Atlantic Republican Tradition* (Princeton, NJ: Princeton University Press, 1975).

Procacci, Giuliano. *Machiavelli nella cultura europea dell'èta moderna* (Bari and Rome: Laterza, 1995).

Putnam, Robert D. *Bowling Alone: The Collapse and Revival of American Community* (New York: Simon & Schuster, 2000).

Raimondi, Ezio. *Politica e commedia; dal Beroaldo al Machiavelli* (Bologna: il Mulino, 1972).

Rebhorn, Wayne A. *Foxes and Lions: Machiavelli's Confidence Men* (Ithaca, NY: Cornell University Press, 1988).

Ridolfi, Roberto. *The Life of Niccolò Machiavelli*, tr. Cecil Grayson (Chicago: University of Chicago Press, 1963).

————. *Studi sulle commedie del Machiavelli* (Pisa: Nistri-Lischi, 1968).

Ruffo-Fiore, Silvia. *Niccolò Machiavelli* (Boston: Twayne, 1982).

Ruggiero, Guido. *Machiavelli in Love* (Baltimore: Johns Hopkins University Press, 2007).

Sasso, Gennaro. *Niccolò Machiavelli: Storia del suo pensiero politico* (Naples: Istituto italiano per gli studi storici, 1958).

————. *Machiavelli e Cesare Borgia: Storia di un giudizio* (Rome: Ateneo, 1966).

————. *Studi su Machiavelli* (Naples: Morano, 1967).

————. *Machiavelli e gli antichi e altri saggi*, 3 vols. (Milan and Naples: Riccardo Ricciardi, 1987).

————. *Niccolò Machiavelli*, 2 vols. (Bologna: Il Mulino, 1993).

Schevill, Ferdinand. *The Medici* (New York: Harper & Row, 1960 [1949]).

Seward, Desmond. *The Burning of the Vanities* (Sutton, 2006).

Skinner, Quentin. *Machiavelli* (New York: Hill & Wang, 1981).

————. *Machiavelli: A Very Short Introduction* (Oxford: Oxford University Press, 1981).

Spirito, Ugo. *Machiavelli e Guicciardini* [4th ed.] (Florence: Sansoni, 1970).

Strauss, Leo. *Thoughts on Machiavelli* (Chicago: University of Chicago Press, 1958).

Struever, Nancy S. *Theory as Practice: Ethical Inquiry in the Renaissance* (Chicago: University of Chicago Press, 1992).

Vidal, Gore. *Inventing a Nation: Washington, Adams, Jefferson* (New Haven, CT: Yale University Press, 2003).

Villari, Pasquale. *The Life and Times of Niccolò Machiavelli*, tr. Linda Villari (London: T. Fisher Unwin, 1898; reprt. Houston: Scholarly Publications, 1972).

Viroli, Maurizio. *From Politics to Reason of State* (New York: Cambridge University Press, 1992).

————. *Machiavelli* (Oxford: Oxford University Press, 1998).

————. *Niccolò's Smile: A Biography of Machiavelli*, tr. Antony Shugaar (New York: Farrar Straus and Giroux, 2000).

Whitfield, J. H. *Machiavelli* (New York: Russell & Russell, 1965).

————. *Discourses on Machiavelli* (Cambridge: W. Heffer, 1969).

Wolf, Naomi. *The End of America: Letter of Warning to a Young Patriot* (White River Junction, VT: Chelsea Green Publishing, 2007).

ARTICLES

Ascoli, Albert Russell. "Pyrrhus's Rules: Playing with Power from Boccaccio to Machiavelli," *Modern Language Notes* 114(1999): 14–57.

Bacchelli, Riccardo. "'Istorico, comico, e tragico,' ovvero Machiavelli artista," *Nuova antologia* 95(1960): 3–20.

Baldan, Paulo. "Sulla vera natura della *Mandragola* e dei suoi personaggi," *Il Ponte* 34(1978): 387–407.

Baldassari, Stefano-Ugo. "Costanti del pensiero machiavelliano nel *Decennale* 1 e nel 'Capitolo della Fortuna,'" *Italian Quarterly* 33(1996): 17–28.

Barber, Joseph A. "La strategia linguistica di Ligurio nella *Mandragola* di Machiavelli," *Italianistica* 13(1984): 387–95.

———. "The Irony of Lucrezia," *Studies in Philology* 82.4(1985): 450–59.

Barberi-Squarotti, Giorgio. "Il Machiavelli fr il 'sublime' della contemplazione intellectuale e il 'comico' della prassi," *Lettere italiane* 21(1969): 129–54.

———. "Storia e etica in versi: Il tono medio del Machiavelli," *Italianistica* 1974: 15–32.

———. "Progetto e prassi: Le 'Operette' del Machiavelli," *Modern Language Notes* 1977:17–38.

Bardazzi, Giovanni. "Techniche narrative nel Machiavelli. scrittore di lettere," *Annali della Scuola Normale Superiore di Pisa: Classe di Lettere e Filosofia* 1975: 1443–89.

Beecher, Donald A. "Machiavelli's *Mandragola* and the Emerging Animateur," *Quaderni d'Italianistica* 5:2(1984): 171–89.

Behuniak-Long, Susan. "The Significance of Lucrezia in Machiavelli's *La mandragola*," *Review of Politics* 51(1989): 264–83.

Bernard, John. "Writing and the Paradox of the Self: Machiavelli's Literary Vocation," *Renaissance Quarterly* 59(2006): 59–89.

Bertelli, Sergio. "When Did Machiavelli Write *Mandragola?*" *Renaissance Quarterly* 24(1980): 317–26.

Bonora, Ettore. "Qualche proposta per il testo e il commento del capitolo di fortuna del Machiavelli," *Giornale di Linguistica Italiano* 105(1988): 321–36.

Boucher, David. "The Duplicitous Machiavelli," *Machiavelli Studies* 3(1990): 163–72.

Cabrini, Anna-Maria. "Intorno al primo *Decennale*," *Rinascimento* 33(1993): 69–89.

Caretti, L. "Machiavelli scrittore," *Terzoprogramma* 1(1970): 49–57.

Carver, Eugene. "Machiavelli and the Politics of Rhetorical Invention," *CLIO* 14:2(1985): 157–78.

Casadei, Alberto. "Su alcuni nuovi studi machiavelliani," *Esperienze Letterarie* 17:3(1992): 65–76.

Chiappelli, Fredi. "Machiavelli as Secretary," *Italian Quarterly* 13(1970): 27–44.

Cioffari, Vincenzo. "The Function of Fortune in Dante, Boccaccio and Machiavelli," *Italica* 24(1947): 1–13.

Clark, Richard C. "Machiavelli: Bibliographical Spectrum," *Review of National Literatures: Italy—Machiavelli, "500,"* 1(1970): 83–135.

Cutinelli-Rengina, Emanuele. "Machiavelli (contro)riformato," *Belfagor* 54.2(1999): 215–25.

D'Amico, Jack. "Three Forms of Character: *Virtù*, *Ordini*, and *Materia* in Machiavelli's *Discorsi*," *Italian Quarterly* 22(1981): 5–13.

————. "The *Virtù* of Women: Machiavelli's *Mandragola* and *Clizia*," *Interpretation* 12(1984): 261–73.

————. "Machiavelli and Ambition," *Italian Quarterly* 34(1997): 5–16.

Della Terza, Dante. "The Most Recent Image of Machiavelli: The Contribution of the Linguist and the Literary Historian," *Italian Quarterly* 13(1970): 91–113.

————. "I proemi del Machiavelli," *Yearbook of Italian Studies* 8(1989): 1–9.

Derla, Luigi. "Machiavelli moralista," *Italianistica* 10:3(1981): 21–35.

Di Maria, Salvatore. "Nicomaco and Sofronia: Fortune and Desire in Machiavelli's *Clizia*," *Sixteenth Century Journal* 14:2(1983): 201–13.

————. "La struttura dialogica nel *Principe*," *Modern Language Notes* 99:1(1984): 65–79.

————. "The Ethical Premises for the *Mandragola*'s New Society," *Italian Culture* 7(1986–89): 17–33.

Dionisotti, Carlo. "Appunti sulla *Mandragola*," *Belfagor* 39:6(1984): 621–44.

Fedi, Francesca. "Personaggi e 'paradossi' nei *Discorsi* Machavelliani," *Lettere Italiane* 50(1998): 485–505.

Ferroni, Giulio. "Le 'cose vane' nelle *Lettere* di Machiavelli," *La rassegna della letteratura italiana* 76(1972): 215–64.

Ferrucci, Frano. "Antropologia machiavelliana," *Annali d'Italianistica* 15(1997): 99–108.

Fido, Franco. "Machiavelli 1469–1969: Politica e teatro nel badalucco di messer Nicia," *Italica* 46(1969): 359–75.

————. "Machiavelli in His Time and Ours," *Italian Quarterly* 13(1970): 3–21.

————. "Appunti sulla memoria letteraria di Machiavelli," *Modern Language Notes* 89(1974): 1–12.

Flaumenhaft, Mera J. "The Comic Remedy: Machiavelli's *Mandragola*," *Interpretation* 7(1978): 33–74.

Fleischer, Martin. "Trust and Deceit in Machiavelli's Comedies," *Journal of the History of Ideas* 27(1966): 368–74.

Geerken, John H. "Homer's Image of the Hero in Machiavelli: A Comparison of Arête and Virtù," *Italian Quarterly* 14(1970): 45–90.

————. "Machiavelli: Magus, Theologian, or Trickster?" *Machiavelli Studies* 3(1990): 95–116.

Gilbert, Felix. "The Humanist Concept of the Prince and *The Prince* of Machiavelli," *Journal of Modern History* 11(1939): 449–65.

————. "The Composition and Structure of Machiavelli's *Discorsi*," *Journal of the History of Ideas* 14(1953): 135–56.

————. "Machiavelli in Modern Historical Scholarship," *Italian Quarterly* 13(1970): 9–26.

Giraldi, Robert. "Machiavelli's *Mandragola*: The Root of Revelry or Rebeldry?" *Canadian Journal of Italian Studies* 15:44(1992): 17–28.

Greene, Thomas Machiavelli. "The End of Discourse in Machiavelli's *Prince*," *Yale French Studies* 67(1984): 57–71.

Gundersheimer, Werner. "San Casciano, 1513: A Machiavellian Moment," *Journal of Medieval and Renaissance Studies* 17(1987): 41–58.

Inglese, Giorgio. "Postille machiavelliane," *La cultura* 23(1985): 517–22.

———. "Audiences and Rhetorical Strategies in Machiavelli, Shakespeare, and Molière," *Comparative Literature Studies* 21:4(1984): 363–82.

Loeffler, Bertina. "Comic Rebirth in Machiavelli's *Prince* and *Clizia*," *Cincinnati Romance Review* 14(1995): 1–7.

Lukes, Timothy. "Fortune Comes of Age (in Machiavelli's Literary Works)," *Sixteenth Century Journal* 9(1980): 35–50.

Maestri, Delmo. "Bandello e Machiavelli: Interesse e riprovazione," *Lettere Italiane* 43:3(1991): 354–3.

———. "Della *Vita di C.C.*, alle *Istorie Fiorentine*," *Rivista di Studi Italiani* 16(1998): 128–46.

Mansfield, Harvey C. "Machiavelli's New Regime," *Italian Quarterly* 13(1970): 63–95.

Marchand, J.-J. "Contributi all'Epistolario Machiavelliano: La lettera al Vettori del 10 dicembre 1514 nel testo originale inedito," *La Bibliofilia* 72(1970): 289–302.

Martelli, Mario. "Schede sulla cultura di Machiavelli," *Interpres* 6(1985–86): 283–330.

Martinez, Ronald L. "The Pharmacy of Machiavelli: Roman Lucretia in *Mandragola*," *Renaissance Drama* 14(1983): 1–43.

Masciandaro, Franco. "I 'castellucci' e i *ghiribizzi*, del Machiavelli epistolografo," *Italica* 46(1969): 135–48.

———. "Machiavelli umorista," *Veltro* 40(1996): 190–95.

Mayer, Thomas F. "Mysterious, Hellacious Machiavelli," *Sixteenth Century Journal* 21:1(1990): 105–9.

Mazzeo, Joseph A. "The Poetry of Power: Machiavelli's Literary Vision," *Review of National Literatures: Italy—Machiavelli, "500,"* 1(1970): 38–62.

McCanles, Michael. "Machiavelli's *Principe* and the Textualization of History," *Modern Language Notes* 97(1982): 1–18.

Najemy, John. "Machiavelli and the Medici: The Lessons of Florentine History," *Renaissance Quarterly* 35(1982): 551–766.

Nederman, Cary J. "Amazing Grace, Fortune, God, and Free Will in Machiavelli's Thought," *Journal of the History of Ideas* 60:4(1999): 617–38.

Olivieri, Mario. "La technica politica nel 'Principe' di Niccolò Machiavelli," *Filosofia* 20(1969): 565–78.

Paden, Michael. "Un'allegoria per Alessandro VI e Monna Belfagor," *Belfagor* 49:1(1994): 65–73.

Padoan, Giorgio. "Il tramonto di Machiavelli," *Lettere italiane* 33(1981): 457–81.

Palmer, Robert, and James F. Pontuso. "The Master Fool: The Conspiracy of Machiavelli's *Mandragola*," *Perspectives on Political Science* 25(1996): 124–31.

Parronchi, Antonio. "La prima rappresentazione della *Mandragola*," *La Bibliofilia* 64(1962): 59–69.

Pesca-Colo, Carmela. *"La Clizia* come meditazione senile di Machiavelli," *Forum Italicum* 28(1994): 252–68.

Pocock, J. G. A. "Machiavelli in the Liberal Cosmos," *Political Theory* 13(1985): 559–74.

Preuss, J. Samuel. "Machiavelli's Functional Analysis of Religion," *Journal of the History of Ideas* 40(1979): 171–90.

Price, Russell. "The Senses of *Virtù* in Machiavelli," *European Studies Review* 3(1973): 315–45.

———. "The Theme of *Gloria* in Machiavelli," *Renaissance Quarterly* 30(1977): 588–631.

Quaglio, Enzo. "Fortuna donna nel *Principe*," *Annali della Scuola Normale Superiore di Pisa: Classe di Lettere e Filosofia* 18:4(1988): 1691–1738.

Raimondi. Ezio. "Il teatro di Machiavelli," *Studi storici* 10(1969): 749–98.

———. "Il sasso del Machiavelli," *Strumenti critici* 9(1970): 86–91.

———. "Machiavelli and the Rhetoric of the Warrior," *Modern Language Notes* 92(1977): 1–16.

Richardson, Brian. "Two Notes on Machiavelli's *Asino*," *Bibliotheque d'Humanisme et Renaissance* 40(1978): 137–41.

Ridolfi, Roberto, and Paolo Ghiglieri. "I *Ghiribizzi* al Soderini," *La bibliofilia* 72(1970): 53–74.

Sasso, Gennaro. "Il celebrato sogno di Machiavelli," *Cultura* 1976: 26–101.

———. "Considerazioni sulla 'Mandragola,'" in Machiavelli, *Mandragola*, (Milan: Rizzoli, 1985 [1980]), pp. 5–18.

Sherberg, Michael. "The Problematics of Reading in Machiavelli's *Discourses*," *Modern Philology* 89:2(1991): 175–95.

Shumer, S. M. "Machiavelli's Republican Politics and Its Corruption," *Political Theory* 7(1979): 5–34.

Skinner, Quentin. "Machiavelli on the Maintenance of Liberty," *Politics* 18(1983): 3–15.

Sparacio, Francesca R. "Il processo del comico ne *La mandragola* di Niccolò Machiavelli," *Romance Review* 5:1(1995): 73–85.

Stefani, Luigina. "Coordinate orizontali nel teatro comico del primo Cinquecento," *Belfagor* 36:3(1981): 275–97.

Sunberg, Theodore A. *"Belfagor:* Machiavelli's Short Story," *Interpretation* 19(1992): 243–50.

Svez, Gerald. "The Enigma of the Political Stage Director," *SubStance* 25(1996): 3–45.

Tarlton, Charles D. *"Fortuna* and the Landscape of Action in Machiavelli's *Prince*," *New Literary History* 30:4(1999): 737–55.

Tylus, Jane. "Theater and Its Social Uses: Machiavelli's *Mandragola* and the Spectacle of Infamy," *Renaissance Quarterly* 53(2000): 656–83.

Vilchez, Patricia. "The Delegate Womb," *American Journal of Italian Studies* 22(1999): 99–125.

Waley, Daniel. "The Primitivist Element in Machiavelli's Thought," *Journal of the History of Ideas* 31(1971): 91–98.

Whitfield, J. H. "Machiavelli and Castruccio," *Italian Studies* 8(1953): 1–28.

———. "On Machiavelli's Use of *Ordine*," *Italian Studies* 10(1955): 19–39.

Wood, Neal. "Machiavelli's Concept of *Virtù* Reconsidered," *Political Studies* 15(1967): 159–72.

Zanini, Adelino. "Machiavelli, l'etico contro il politico," *Belfagor* 39:1(1984): 31–40.

CHAPTERS IN BOOKS

Aquilecchia, G. "La favola *mandragola* si chiama," in *Collected Essays on Italian Language and Literature Presented to Dr. Kathleen Speight*, pp. 73–100.

Ascoli, Albert Russell. "Machiavelli and the Gift of Counsel," in *Machiavelli and the Discourse of Literature*, pp. 245–53.

Barberi-Squarotti, G. "L'arduo piacere del narrare," in Machiavelli, *Belfagor arcidiavolo*, pp. 41–48.

Berlin, Isaiah. "The Originality of Machiavelli," in *Studies on Machiavelli*, pp. 147–206.

Bertelli, Sergio. "Machiavelli e la politica esterna fiorentina," in *Studies on Machiavelli*, pp. 29–72.

Carroll, Linda. "Machiavelli's Veronese Prostitute: *Venetia Figurata*," in *Gender Rhetorics*, pp. 93–106.

Celse, Mirielle. "La Beffa chez Machiavel, dramaturge et conteur," in *Formes et significations de la "Beffa*," pp. 99–110.

Dionisotti, Carlo. "Appunti su capitoli di Machiavelli," in *Collected Essays on Italian Language and Literature Presented to Kathleen Speight*, pp. 55–71.

———. "Machiavelli letterato," in *Studies on Machiavelli*, pp. 101–3.

———. "Machiavelli, man of Letters," in *Machiavelli and the Discourse of Literature*, pp. 16–51.

Fazion, Paolo. "*L'Asino* da leggere," in Gian Mario Anselmi and P. Fazion, *Machiavelli: L'Asino e le bestie*, pp. 25–134.

Ferroni, Giulio. "'Transformation' and 'Mutation' in Machiavelli's *Mandragola*," in *Machiavelli and the Discourse of Literature*, pp. 81–116.

———. "Appunti sull'*Asino* di Machiavelli," in *Letteratura e critica: studi in onore di Natalino Sapegno*, pp. 313–45.

Fido, Franco. "Politica e teatro nel badalucco di messer Nicia," in Fido, *La metamorfosi del centauro*, pp. 91–108.

———. "L'esule e il centauro: Emblemi e memoria in Machiavelli," in Fido, *La metamorfosi del centauro*, pp. 109–22.

Flanagan, Thomas. "The Concept of *Fortuna* in Machiavelli," in *The Political Calculus*, pp. 137–54.

Gilbert, Felix. "Machiavelli: The Renaissance of the Art of War," in E. M. Earle, ed., *The Makers of Modern Strategy*, pp. 11–31.

————. "Machiavelli's *Istorie fiorentine*: An Essay in Interpretation," in *Studies on Machiavelli*, pp. 73–99.

Grazzini, Filippo. "Machiavelli, Guicciardini e le regole di un gioco epistolare," in *Passare il tempo*, pp. 651–64.

Greenwood, Richard. "Machiavelli and the Problem of Human Inflexibility," in *The Cultural Heritage of the Italian Renaissance*, pp. 196–214.

Harvey, Michael. "Lost in the Wilderness: Love and Longing in *L'Asino*," in *The Comedy and Tragedy of Machiavelli*, pp. 120–37.

Lorch, Maristella de Panizza. "Confessore e chiesa in tre commedie del Rinascimento: *Philogenia, Mandragola, Cortegiana*," in *Il teatro italiano del Rinascimento*, pp. 301–48.

————. "Women in the Context of Machiavelli's *Mandragola*," in *Donna: Women in Italian Culture*, pp. 253–71.

Lord, Carnes. "Allegory in Machiavelli's *Mandragola*," in *Political Philosophy and the Human Soul*, pp. 152–67.

Martelli, Mario. "Per un dittico mano," in Niccolò Machiavelli, *Novella di Belfagor, L'Asino*, pp. 7–42.

Martinez, Ronald L. "Benefit of Absence: Machiavellian Valediction in *Clizia*," in *Machiavelli and the Discourse of Literature*, pp. 117–44.

————. "Tragic Machiavelli," in *The Comedy and Tragedy of Machiavelli*, pp. 102–19.

Matteucci, Nicola. "Niccolò Machiavelli, politologo," in *Studies on Machiavelli*, pp. 207–46.

Minogue, K. R. "Theatricality and Politics: Machiavelli's Concept of *Fantasia*," in *The Morality of Politics*," ed. Bhikha Parekh and R. N. Becki, pp. 148–62.

Najemy, John. "Machiavelli. and Geta: Men of Letters," in *Machiavelli and the Discourse of Literature*, pp. 53–80.

Pampaloni, Guido. "Il Movimento Piagnone secondo la Lista del 1497," in *Studies on Machiavelli*, pp. 335–48.

Paolucci, Anne. "Livy's Lucretia, Shakespeare's 'Lucrece,' Machiavelli's *Mandragola*," in *Il teatro italiano del Rinascimento*, pp. 619–35.

Perez, Tiziano. "*Reputazione* in Machiavelli's Thought," in *Machiavelli: Figure-Reputation*, pp. 165–77.

Pincin, Carlo. "Osservazioni sul modo de procedere di Machiavelli nei Discorsi," in *Renaissance Studies in Honor of Hans Baron*, ed. Anthony Molho and J. A. Tedeschi, pp. 385–408.

Plamenetz, John. "In Search of Human *Virtù*," in *The Political Calculus*, pp. 157–78.

Raimondi, Ezio. "Il veleno della *Mandragola*," in *Politica e commedia*, pp. 253–64.

Rubenstein, Nicolai. "Machiavelli and the World of Florentine Politics," in *Studies on Machiavelli*, pp. 3–28.

Ruggiero, Guido. "Machiavelli in Love: The Self-presentation of an Aging Lover," in *Machiavelli in Love*, pp. 108–62.

Schiesari, Juliana. "Libidinal Economies: Machiavelli and Fortune's Rape," in *Desire in the Renaissance*, pp. 169–83.

Sereno, Renzo. "A Falsification by Machiavelli," in *Psychoanalysis and History*, ed. Bruce Mazlich, pp. 108–14.

Siegel, J. E. "Violence and Order in Machiavelli," in *Violence and Aggression in the History of Ideas*, ed. Phillip P. Wiener and John Fisher, pp. 49–64.

Tarantino, Maurizio. *"L'Asino* e la satira politica," in *Niccolò Machiavelli: Politico storico letterato*, pp. 131–36.

Tavani, Giuseppe. "Niccolò Machiavelli e Franceso Vettori: Le riflessioni politiche attraverso l'epistolario," in *Machiavelli. attuale/machiavel actuel*, pp. 75–86.

Tonelli, Franco. "Machiavelli's *Mandragola* and the Signs of Power," in *Drama, Sex, and Politics*, pp. 35–54.

Vanossi, L. "Situazione e sviluppi del teatro machiavelliano," in *Lingua e strutture del teatro italiano del Rinascimento*, pp. 3–108.

Ulysse, G. "Un conteur inachevé: notes sur la correspondance de Machiavelli," in *La correspondance*, pp. 49–80.

Weinstein, Donald. "Machiavelli and Savonarola," in *Studies on Machiavelli*, pp. 251–64.

Whitfield, J. H. "Considerazioni pratiche sui *Discorsi*," in *Studies on Machiavelli*, pp. 361–69.

Zuckert, Catherine. "Fortune Is a Woman—But So Is Prudence: Machiavelli's *Clizia*," in *Finding a New Feminism*, pp. 24–35.

CRITICAL ANTHOLOGIES

Collected Essays on Italian Language and Literature Presented to Dr. Kathleen Speight (New York: Manchester University Press/Barnes & Noble, 1971).

The Comedy and Tragedy of Machiavelli: Essays on the Literary Works, ed. Vickie B. Sullivan (New Haven, CT: Yale University Press, 2000).

La correspondance (edition, fonctions, signification) (Aix-en-Provence: Université de Provence, 1984).

Cultura e scuola 9(1970). Special number on Machiavelli centenary.

The Cultural Heritage of the Italian Renaissance, ed. C. F. J. Griffiths and R. Hastings (Lewiston, NY: Mellen, 1993).

Desire in the Renaissance: Psychoanalysis and Literature, ed. Valeria Finucci and Regina Schwartz (Princeton, NJ: Princeton University Press, 1994).

Donna: Women in Italian Culture, ed. Ada Testaferri (Ottawa: Dovehouse, 1989).

Drama, Sex, and Politics, ed. James Redmond (Cambridge: Cambridge University Press, 1985).

Finding a New Feminism: Rethinking the Woman Question for Liberal Democracy, ed. Pamela Jensen (Lanham, MD: Rowman & Littlefield, 1996).

Formes et significations de la "Beffa" dans la littérature italienne de la renaissance (Paris: University de la Sorbonne Nouvelle, 1972).

Gender Rhetorics: Postures of Dominance and Submission in History, ed. Richard C. Trexler (Binghamton, NY: Medieval and Renaissance Texts and Studies, 1994).

Lingua e strutture del teatro italiano del Rinascimento (Padua: Liviana, 1970).

Machiavelli: Cynic, Patriot, or Political Scientist? ed. De Lamar Jensen (Boston: D. C. Heath, 1960).

Machiavelli: Figure-Reputation, ed. Joep Leersen and Menno Spiering (Amsterdam: Rodopi, 1996).

Machiavelli and Republicanism, ed. Gisela Bock, Q. Skinner, and M. Viroli (Cambridge: Cambridge University Press, 1990).

Machiavelli and the Discourse of Literature, ed. Albert Russell Ascoli and Victoria Kahn (Ithaca, NY: Cornell University Press, 1993).

Machiavelli attuale/Machiavel actuel, ed. Georges Barthoni (Ravella: Longo, 1982).

Machiavelli in Love: Sex, Self, and Society in the Italian Renaissance (Baltimore: Johns Hopkins University Press, 2007).

The Makers of Modern Strategy, ed. E. M. Earle (Princeton, NJ: Princeton University Press, 1944).

The Morality of Politics, ed. Bhiku Parekh and R. N. Berki (London: Allen & Unwin, 1972).

Niccolò Machiavelli: Politico storico letterato, ed. J. J. Marchand (Rome: Salerno, 1997).

Passare il tempo: Atti del Convegno di Pienza (Rome: Salerno, 1993).

The Political Calculus, ed. Anthony Parel (Toronto: University of Toronto Press, 1972)

Political Philosophy and the Human Soul, ed. Michael Palmer and T. Pangle (Lanham, MD: Rowman & Littlefield, 1994).

Psychoanalysis and History, ed. Bruce Mazlich (New York: Universal Library, 1960).

Renaissance Studies in Honor of Hans Baron, ed. Anthony Molho and J. A. Tedeschi (DeKalb: Northern Illinois University Press, 1971).

Il Rinascimento: Aspetti e problemi attuali, ed. Vittore Braca *et al.* (Florence: Olschki, 1982).

Studies on Machiavelli, ed. Myron P. Gilmore (Florence: Sansoni, 1972).

Il teatro italiano del Rinascimento, ed. Mariastella Lorch (Milan: Edizioni di Comunità, 1980).

Violence and Aggression in the History of Ideas, ed. Phillip P. Wiener and John Fisher (New Brunswick, NJ: Rutgers University Press, 1974).

INDEX

About the Author

JOHN BERNARD received his Ph.D. from the University of Minnesota and is the author of *Vergil at 2000: Commemorative Essays on the Poet and His Influence* (1986) and *Ceremonies of Innocence: Pastoralism in the Poetry of Edmund Spenser* (1989).